Survival
in the Outdoors

Survival
in the Outdoors

Byron Dalrymple

Illustrated by
Charles Waterhouse
Carl Sigman
Fergus Retrum

OUTDOOR LIFE · E. P. DUTTON & CO., INC.
NEW YORK

Library of Congress Catalog Card Number: 71-167606

Ninth Printing, 1979

Designed by Jeff Fitschen

Manufactured in the United States of America

Contents

**Survival
in the Outdoors**

1 / *Orientation for Survival*

INVARIABLY when survival is discussed, people think of a lost man trying to survive. To be sure, a number of persons venturing into the outdoors do become lost each year. But the idea of survival does not begin and end there. *Survival situations may occur even when you are not lost.*

Heading out on a jaunt, you probably don't think at all of any danger. Why should you? You've been on outdoor trips time after time. If you are going into a large region sparsely settled, you are cautioned undoubtedly not to get lost. But a great many other situations might arise that will suddenly place you in a position where you must, by your own astuteness, get out of a difficulty of survival proportions.

When You Are Not Lost

Not long ago, for example, only a short distance from one of the largest cities in the Southwest, a group of five persons, children and adults, perished in the desert. Their vehicle had become stuck. They were not lost. All they had to do, and failed to do, was stay in its shade. Water was within a third of a mile, a paved highway only a quarter-hour on foot. They used improper judgment and did not have necessary, simple knowledge. Heat and exposure needlessly killed them.

Consider your transportation into any wilderness region, or for that matter into any wild but not necessarily far-removed region. You can backpack, ride a horse, use a motor vehicle such as 4WD, trail bike, or snowmobile. You can travel by plane or by boat. You may be an expert woodsman who realizes that emergencies can arise. And the emergency may have no bearing upon your expertness or ineptness.

Let us say that you are alone, backpacking, and you are suddenly snowed in. Or you injure a leg. Or you are riding a horse and it falls and breaks a leg. Perhaps you are in a motor vehicle and it breaks down. Or your trail bike has two ruined tires. Or the boat you used to get thirty miles back in the bush somehow gets cracked up. Or a plane crashes.

It is probable that in all but the plane situation you are not lost at all. But you do have to extricate yourself. Can you do it? Will you be *equipped* to do it, mentally as well as with basic gear? Physically, too? The majority of average outdoorsmen, even those who are deskbound most of the year, are tougher physically than they think, if they can control their mental state and use careful—and practiced—judgment to arrive at a sensible, cautious course of action.

Too much nonsense has been written about this subject. It is fine to know how to build a water-gathering trap in the desert. It is great to know that cattail roots are good to eat. However, the "there's-nothing-to-it-take-heart" bit has lured many a befuddled amateur woodsman into difficulty.

Knowing Yourself

In my opinion, a broad category of survival lore begins with *you,* not with the cattail roots. Again, all of the woods lore is excellent to have, but a man who knows what survival is all about realizes that it begins and ends, really, in his own thinking processes. You can live longer than you think without food or on very little. The specifics of living off the country, making yourself comfortable and safe in emergency situations, and all the information needed to assist you in times of outdoor difficulty are important, but you can't live very long without using your head and knowing how to use it with firm discipline!

An honest evaluation of your mental and physical reactions and capabilities will help you to *cope with yourself*. This is the person, remember—you—who may well be the only one upon whom you can depend to surmount the emergency!

Perhaps you get lost easily. If so, don't be embarrassed. Don't pretend you don't. That's just asking for trouble. As a matter of fact, there are in my experience only three general classes of outdoorsmen so far as orientation is concerned. One type never gets lost, compass or none. I know several of these, but they are rare. Another is what might be termed "pretty good." Look out for these! They're real trouble! Third comes my class, the ones who long ago learned to rely on compass and map. Since I know I am one of these, I don't let myself get into situations where I must depend on my own sense of orientation.

You should know so much about *you* that in any situation of emergency you will be able to predict how you will react. For instance, does altitude bother you? Many people have startling reactions to altitude, mostly caused by low oxygen supply, but also by various phobias, the awesome expanses of mountains, high places and so on. I know precisely how high I can go before I begin to feel some kind of peculiar anxiety. I *know* it will occur, so I don't worry. Also, I know precisely at what altitude I begin to "run out of gas." At ten to twelve thousand feet I do not sleep well, my muscles ache and I never feel top notch. Often a shot of oxygen, a whiff from a portable container taken along, is an immense relief, indeed, a cure.

What happens to you when you enter dense thickets? Have you tried it and do you know? Some persons, though in no real danger, have such severe feelings of claustrophobia in such circumstances that they are physically ill. Others are only slightly discomfited, or not at all. People are indeed individuals.

What happens to your feet on a long hike? Supposedly, if your boots are proper and fit correctly and your socks are not mended or rent, your feet should not be troublesome. But certain persons literally suffer anguish from much steady hiking. The legs of others chronically give out on even a short climb. Very slow going with rest stops every few steps may well be the answer to such a problem. The point is, will you remember these things under strain of emergency?

There are also scores of outdoorsmen who admit to minor or major feelings of panic when they are left alone in the woods or any wild area. It is revealing to know what happens all too often to people who panic. They do strange and totally unreasonable things. A breakdown of a vehicle sends a panicked man off across a swamp instead of down the trail toward help. A hunter who is lost throws away his gun, races through brush, tearing his clothes to shreds. People in panic have been known to cross paved highways and keep on going. They are literally temporarily insane. There are instances of lost men actually hiding from their rescuers.

Don't deny these feelings to yourself. You don't have to dwell on them and enhance their importance. But if you admit them to yourself, and in certain cases even to a guide who is with you, a first step has been made toward dodging trouble.

Survival Mentality

Any practicing and dedicated outdoorsman should form the habit of thinking of himself on all trips as always close to possible emergency. I do not mean that you should go about cowering and frightened, wondering what awful crisis is going to shape up, but you can prepare yourself mentally to realize that emergencies can occur.

Among most primitive peoples *worry* and *panic* as we know them are almost unknown. These peoples are stoic, fatalistic, and usually able to cope with whatever situation occurs, because they are much more familiar with their surroundings than we. The "calm mind of the primitives" is without any question the most important tool that *you* can use in extricating yourself from any emergency. It is so important that the lack of it may tip the balance toward life or death. This is the precise time *not* to let fear and panic grab you. It is a good idea, under many circumstances, to forget about your starting point. Tell yourself there is no hurry about getting back to that place. Where you are now is what's important, and your mental attitude under stress is what will make it possible, or impossible, to eventually return to your original position.

One of the best insurances against panic is to be well-informed beforehand as to just what sort of box you might get yourself into. If you have guts enough to face the truth, there are plenty of emergencies that are downright sticky. Being lost is one of them, because in so many people this particular emergency does induce panic and unfounded fears. Getting yourself out of serious emergencies is not simple, and it certainly isn't always easy or comfortable. You don't just pick a few berries, dig a hole and hit a cold spring, and have fun. Emergencies are too often true ordeals. You want to realize this and keep it always in mind, the better to control yourself if one occurs.

On the bright side, though survival may not be easy,

it is generally possible. If you understand that fact well beforehand, you are preparing your mind for the moment when the sudden realization hits home that you are in trouble. And, though you know it isn't going to be fun, you should try to acquire the attitude that when it happens it *can* be an *adventure*. In fact, it can be the greatest adventure of your life because the stakes are high and the reason for winning so great. How could there be any circumstance in which winning would be of greater consequence, or of more satisfaction!

There were times years ago in this country when wilderness emergencies were far more serious than they are today. One of the most reassuring thoughts any outdoorsman can carry with him is the knowledge that regardless of what variety of emergency turns up, he is almost certain to be found and helped within a short time. *But only if he does his part properly.* In almost all true wilderness regions today, and in many not remote, search and rescue teams are trained and on standby. State agencies such as game and fish departments are equipped with planes and helicopters, and their personnel, both wardens and wildlife biologists, know every square mile of their state or province intimately. In National Forests, the rangers are likewise informed. In serious emergencies, federal agencies such as the Army and Air Corps join in.

Keep solidly in mind that the one thing that will make the work of rescue personnel most difficult will be the errors committed by the person who is in difficulty. *Your* help is as important and probably more so than theirs. You cannot assist others to assist you if you panic. So, whatever difficulty you have got into, don't act immediately or impulsively. *Stay right where you are,* sit down and get hold of yourself. That is the first and most important act.

I have a friend who has spent a great deal of time in wilderness areas of the outdoors. He once told me that whenever he is in a tight spot his first step is to build a fire.

"Even on a hot day in midsummer and in desert-type terrain," he says, "if there is any available material for a fire, I build one. This gives me something to do for a few minutes to get my nerves in shape, rather than sitting and fretting. Also, there is something about a fire that is like 'home.' It is probably a primitive instinct. Where your fire is, that's camp. That's where you belong. After the fire is going, I sit down beside it and begin to plot my course. By then I am calm."

Feeling at home, then, regardless of emergency, is a vital step in winning the battle for survival. Consider that a moment before this emergency arose, you were happy and enjoying life. You might have been lost for some time, but you didn't realize it and so you were not afraid or anxious. But suddenly you realize your situation. This is indeed a jolt. But what has changed? Nothing except your mental attitude. Don't let it run away with you! When you are lost, you are only temporarily removed from the place where you belong *most of the time.* If you have taken with you the proper knowledge, and the proper basic equipment, and you now hang tight to your proper mental attitude, you simply have a problem to work out.

Being Prepared

For years now I have done my best to be prepared for emergencies, not just mentally, but with useful items of equipment as well. The gear you take along must bear a sensible relationship to where you are going, the type of transport you will utilize, and how long you will be gone.

For example, when my boys and I go to our ranch for a day of hunting, we never worry about food or comfort. In an old house on the property we have some cheap iron cots. Occasionally when a hard rain comes, the creek is so high that we can't get out and nobody can get in, until it runs down. So we keep a few canned goods there. We also have a couple of caches under rocks here and there that contain, in tightly sealed glass jars, salt and matches.

We have several old-fashioned cane poles stashed, with lines and hooks attached. On occasion we've caught fish, built a fire, broiled the fish on sticks, salted them and had a meal when we were famished and waiting for the creek to run down. These measures are not actually survival measures. I used them only to illustrate the basic idea. Stretch this remote ranch situation to the true wilderness, and the same philosophy of preparedness applies.

We will discuss various gear specifically in another chapter. But here let me say that I would not pack in by vehicle, horse, boat or plane anywhere without thinking beforehand of how I could get out *without* transportation. On some trips this may mean squirreling away a full-blown backpack outfit suited to the place and the time of year. In fact, that's an easy way to pack most of your gear. In other situations it may be enough to toss in a small rucksack with a few basics for overnight comfort or an afternoon's hike.

Fatigue

Old-fashioned fatigue, exhaustion, is probably one of the main causes of outdoor difficulties. A trout fisherman stays too long on the stream, until he can hardly lift his casting arm. Coming out he stumbles, falls and hits his head on a rock. A hunter going back to camp is so weary he can hardly stay upright. Eager to get in, he stumbles hurriedly along, and tumbles off a ledge and down a shale slide. A backpacker keeps on the trail for so many hours that his senses are dulled. Just tired, all of them. Dangerously tired. Fatigue slows reactions and can even lead to hallucinations. It furthers carelessness: you miss an obscure trail because you don't see it; you're not alert.

There is no valid reason for becoming overtired outdoors, although nearly everyone does it. Know your limits and stay within them. After all, being outdoors is supposed to be for enjoyment. When it ceases to be, and you are in trouble, it is even *more* important not to get overtired. Conserve your energy. Exhaustion is one more difficulty, and it leads to others.

Emergency is always possible, wherever you go. It's like the rock that remains precariously balanced for many years. One day it topples. I don't travel hoping for emergency, or worried over one. I just go ready—

and reasonably confident because I am ready! Perhaps this sounds as if I'm trying to frighten you. But it might be an excellent idea if more people who find recreation in the outdoors were frightened a bit. Once past that state, they begin to work toward preparedness, and the prepared outdoorsman doesn't need to be frightened. He knows how to take charge!

2 / Pre-Emergency Schooling: Learning to Observe

PRE-EMERGENCY schooling for any outdoorsman means learning how to observe: how to look, listen, and correctly interpret what you see and hear. The rifleman who learns how to judge range accurately in either mountains or plains can judge how far it is from landmark to landmark when he travels. If he is adept at using a binocular, or a scope on his rifle, he can spot something distant, raise the glass and place it "right on" instantly. It is surprising how many beginners cannot do this.

To the schooled observer, nothing in the terrain escapes notice. He can go into strange territory and in a few hours be perfectly at home. He has checked out various landmarks and the general direction of watershed flow. He has observed the most common types of vegetation, and whether for example there is a good blueberry or acorn crop this season. He has noted tracks and filed away mentally what made them. He sees where a deer or elk has been bedded, and where a black bear has clawed a stump apart or broken low limbs on chokecherry scrub to get the fruit. If he is fishing along a stream, he soon knows whether or not the ruffed grouse or woodcock are plentiful there.

> Watch for animal tracks in strange country and determine what made them. By identifying the deer tracks here, you would have clues to the vegetation and geography of the area.

Nothing escapes him. Even a small broken branch beside the trail means something and he pauses to assess its meaning.

I said earlier that there are three classes of outdoorsmen so far as orientation is concerned: those who rarely get lost, those who are just "pretty good," and those who get lost easily. Now it is a fact that some outdoorsmen have a better sense of direction than others. But in most cases the person who just can't be lost not only has an excellent natural directional feeling but is mainly, and more importantly, a topnotch observer.

Who Is 'Accident Prone'?

I am sure everyone has heard of what are known as "accident prone" individuals. Are you one? Have you ever thought carefully about this?

I have a close friend who is an avid and very experienced outdoorsman. Once when I was hunting deer with him he fell in rocks, smashed the stock of his rifle and cut his palm so badly that numerous stitches had to be taken. He was hurrying. On another occasion he shot a rifle that had a bullet from a handload stuck in the chamber—it had come loose—and he rammed another home atop it and blew up the gun. By a great miracle he was not killed, but he was seriously injured. He has fallen off a trail horse onto rocks, been hospitalized with pneumonia after being caught in a blizzard while trying to get out of the wilderness back country. These are just a few of his accidents.

So his family calls him accident prone. Even his doctor has sagely agreed that this man has "it" always hanging over him. But I'll tell you something. I have been with this man on a number of occasions under wilderness conditions. And I won't ever go again, regardless of our friendship. The term "accident prone" is purely and simply an excuse.

There is no proof that any man is headed for continuous "accidents" because of his genes. The man I used as an illustration *is* accident-prone, you bet. And I'll tell you why. He is incautious, reckless, inept in judgment, overconfident, has too quick a temper, and though he is a delightful companion most times, he totally lacks good sense and good judgment. Astrologers believe that all this is in the stars, but as this is beyond proof, I will claim emphatically that for every "accident prone" person you show me, I will show you one —the same one—who has somehow not learned about *caution,* one in whose head nothing clicks that says, "Watch it, this can be trouble!" when trouble is standing smack in the path just begging to be dodged!

Some professional guides, more's the pity, are like this. Maybe you recognize yourself. Are you one of these? Are you foreordained to follow a path where boulders fall on your head, vipers appear from nowhere to smite you, holes suddenly yawn in the trail to snap your bones? Cheer up! You can be cured—by you! Fit yourself out to dodge emergencies and chances of having to cope with them are far less.

Some time ago a fisherman out in Aransas Bay on the Texas Gulf coast pulled his boat up to an oil installation platform, climbed up on it to fish. The boat got free and drifted off. The man, in his fifties, decided to swim after it. He drowned. Accident prone? This poor man was simply unbelievably incautious. All he had to do was sit still. He would have been found by boat or Coast Guard plane within minutes after he was missed.

All you have to do is learn what *caution* is all about, school yourself to see an emergency in the making, and *become* cautious and discerning. Think ahead. Do you

In desert terrain, the practiced outdoorsman looking for a campsite stays clear of dry washes and walks in the hottest, brightest sunlight as a safeguard against snakes.

really *need* to drive that go-anywhere 4WD up that especially precarious trail? Recently in Colorado several people rolled with theirs some hundreds of feet and several were killed. The sheep or elk you're going after isn't worth your life. If you can't judge what is truly safe, be smart enough to doubt. Don't take the chance.

So, the first lesson in pre-emergency schooling is to *see* possibilities and avoid emergencies. I've watched hunters walk in places they shouldn't, where a fall would have been serious trouble. I've watched them walk, in hot snake country, in the shady spots, whereas they should have been skirting these and staying in the patches of hottest, brightest sun. I've seen campers set up on gravel bars in streams during rainy seasons—one not long ago when the river rose seven feet in a few hours. The people made it to shore in time, but with not much to spare. I've also seen campers, in desert-mountain country, make camp in a dry wash, an open invitation to disaster even without a drop of rain falling on them. A heavy, distant rainfall on a dry slope could send a wall of water down on them.

Training Your Interest in Nature

Some outdoorsmen are better natural observers than others. But all can learn to be sharp at it. You have to have a keen interest in all of nature, or else train yourself to have it. You must make a conscious effort to know the birds, plants, animals. And you have to make a conscious effort to see everything that goes on around you. It is absolutely amazing to me how deficient many outdoorsmen are in basic knowledge. What good does it do to know that certain plants are edible and nutritious if you don't have any idea what they look like or in what terrains or plant communities they grow? Of what value is it to know that certain woods are far better than others for emergency fires, if you can't identify the trees?

Several years ago, two young fellows in the Southwest, supposedly good outdoorsmen, got themselves into a jam with a 4WD vehicle and spent several exceedingly uncomfortable and hungry days getting out to civilization. They had a shotgun but their only shells were fine birdshot. They debated about trying to bag a deer for food. They said a waterhole near the vehicle was peppered with small deer tracks. But they decided they'd never get close enough to a deer to kill it with birdshot.

What they had actually seen were javelina tracks. This was verified by the people who eventually got their vehicle out. Javelina tracks do superficially resemble the tracks of fawns or small deer. But the hoof sections are rounded in front, and uneven. To a trained observer in the desert, they are unmistakable. All the two had to do was sit by the waterhole and wait. The birdshot would have knocked over a small javelina. It has been done on numerous occasions.

Learning to observe is not only important to the "sometime" when trouble may appear, it is also a grand means of outdoor entertainment and to the accomplished a matter of immense pride.

I have two friends, brothers, whom I consider among the best outdoor observers I know. I don't believe these gentlemen will ever get into serious outdoor difficulty. I have been with them in Canada, Mexico, the western mountains, the southwestern deserts. They see everything, hear everything. I have watched them check out a bad piece of trail to see whether or not their 4WD would be able to negotiate it, and exactly how the bad spot should be approached. I've watched them turn

When you travel by vehicle, stop and look over difficult spots of trail before continuing. It's better to detour than to risk serious breakdown.

down a good many such spots. They knew it would be foolhardy because of the type of soil, or the lack of anything to attach a winch cable to. When we hike anywhere together they are always *looking back*. Sure you know what the landmark you are heading toward

Even on short forays, look over your shoulder often to see what the landmark just passed will look like on the return trip.

looks like as you approach it, but how will it look when you're returning? The only way you can tell is to look back at it, and put into your mind how it appears from this side. Watching your back trail even on short jaunts where no big trouble but only brief inconvenience might occur, is the least practiced yet one of the most important acts of the observant outdoorsman. In wilderness situations *it is absolutely crucial!*

Sounds and Smells

In addition to visual images, no sounds should go unnoticed. In a forest, the distant snarl of a chain saw has a message. It is also a directional point. A hunter lost in Wisconsin several years ago heard one plainly, he recalled later, the morning he went out but forgot about it after he became confused. There was a timber-cutting operation within less than a mile of him. The sound of traffic on a main highway, apt to be heavier in daytime, but likely to have loud big-truck sounds at night, is a sound to stow away for future reference. A friend of mine in Minnesota heard a distant "thud, thud, thud" partially obscured by a whimsical breeze. He took time to get on a knoll where he could hear better. He had wrecked his canoe on a float trip and needed help. The sound, as he evaluated it, just had to be someone chopping wood. It could be a camp. He took a compass bearing as closely as possible on it, knowing it probably wouldn't last long and that it could not be heard if it were very far away. It was a camp of fishermen on a small nearby lake and he walked right to it.

You should constantly listen for animal and bird sounds and learn what they mean. A hooting blue grouse, a rather naive species, in early spring could mean food to a desperate man. The sound of small pikas or coneys, those tiny rabbit-like animals of the high peaks, going "beep, beep" early and late, could lead to needed food in a bad situation, but only if the listener knows what makes the sound.

Perhaps you have never thought about it, but even a practiced sense of *smell* and an awareness that many smells are easily identifiable in the outdoor world can be of value. While hunting into the wind you can catch the scent of such animals as deer or elk, especially in the rut, and droves of javelina, from surprising distances. Patches of ripe strawberries give off a delectable and identifiable odor. So do several other varieties of wild fruits.

You should always be alert to the smell of smoke. It may mean a forest fire, or a campfire. A keenly attuned student of nature can smell a rattlesnake den when the snakes first come out in spring. It is even possible to smell spawning fish from a lakeshore or from a boat, when large concentrations, such as bluegills or other shallow-water spawners, are on their beds.

To be sure, many such scents may not have anything to do with survival, but again, *one might*. Having all of your senses alert at all times, trying constantly to learn and identify, builds up a storehouse of knowledge that may have endless uses. But more than that, the outdoorsman who approaches experience in every conceivable way is the one who is likely to be the most resourceful when the chips are down.

Nature lore is endless. The latitude and terrain have infinite bearing on it. I recall sitting with the two brothers previously mentioned in an evening camp in strange territory in a brushy area of the Southwest. We were listening to coyotes howling. They seemed especially plentiful.

"Must be a good year for rabbits," one of them remarked.

It was. Predator numbers rise and fall with the cycles of their forage. Sighting many hawks always means that the area has rodents and rabbits in abundance. Knowing the time of year when various crops of wild foods, from cactus fruits to wild persimmons to piñon nuts, are ripe is valuable. Even a knowledge of the times of year where certain species of fish spawn, especially those that run from lake into streams, is important. For example, in northern streams tributary to lakes, suckers jam by thousands even into small creeks. This occurs about the middle of May in northern Canada, earlier farther south. Smelt runs pack certain small creeks shortly after ice out. Both suckers and smelt under these conditions can be caught or flipped out on the bank by hand. Trout of several varieties, some of which spawn in spring and others in fall, can be trapped in small feeders by jerry-built small dams and caught by hand.

It will not do you much good to begin boning up on nature lore *after* you are in difficulty. Nor do you have to wait until you are on a wilderness trip to start. When you go pheasant hunting on somebody's farm, or trout fishing for a couple of hours along a stream close to which you have parked your car, keep fully alert. Practice. Look, listen and interpret. Every sight and sound in the environment is important to the whole, and important to you if you are to be fully at home in it. Learning and checking the authenticity of your observations is also most enjoyable. You see things no one else sees. You hear things your partners don't. You read signs they don't even see.

This recalls a hunt I made one season for Gambel's quail, those handsomely plumed desert runners. We were in desert country totally new to me, but I was with a native who knew it well. He kept stopping the car and getting out to check various places that might be used by quail. At first I didn't catch on to what he was doing. Finally he returned and got his dog out on leash.

"There's a good bunch around here somewhere," he said.

Suddenly I knew. He was checking for quail *tracks*. It was the first time I had ever heard of anybody looking for quail by their tracks. But in this soil and with sparse vegetation they were easy to see. He knew that quail coveys do not range widely. Birds were somewhere within a quarter mile of us.

Reading Correctly

As you learn to read all of the sights and sounds around you, be certain your *interpretation* of what you see is correct. A somewhat amusing incident occurred one fall in Utah when I visited with a hunter who was after mule deer. It was early in the season, and I was headed with some other hunters for the high country and the aspen stands. The weather had been mild and the deer had not come down to the foothills yet. But this hunter insisted he was working an area where there were swarms of deer. They were, he told us, too smart for him. He had yet to see his first one.

We took time to look at this "hot" area. He had found plenty of sign, sure enough. Piles of droppings were scattered everywhere. But unfortunately in the dry air of this country the droppings do not change much in appearance, especially if damp from dew or a shower, over a long period. He was hunting the lower country winter range of the deer, and the sign was from the previous winter!

In a later chapter we will discuss weather in some detail. Along with other nature lore, bear in mind that weather is part of it. You should always be keenly aware of what the weather is doing, and what you suspect the signs mean it may do. I have traveled with many old-time "weather hands" who would say, "I don't like the feel of that wind." Or, "That breeze has got the smell of rain on it. Let's get out of here." Total awareness can be practiced and learned, and it is invaluable.

So, on every trip you make, no matter how short, practice being what is generally called a "good woodsman," even if you're just hunting cottontails on your back forty. The man who never cares about knowing one bush from another, who never sees tracks or feels a storm coming is almost certain to find himself in trouble when he needs such information. Conversely, the careful, sharp observer who has always schooled himself will be ready for that day when he may need all senses keenly honed, when what he sees and hears and properly interprets may be the very means to his survival.

3 / Where Emergencies May Occur

A NUMBER of outdoor-minded people pursue activities other than hunting and fishing. Some are rock hounds. Some backpack just for sheer enjoyment of wilderness hiking. A few make canoe trips or travel by rubber boats on remote rivers and lakes. Nonetheless, by far the majority of outdoorsmen who get into the back country are sportsmen, fishermen and hunters. These millions meet the most challenges by mass of numbers alone and face the possibilities of a major share of emergencies.

With transport so efficient today, thousands of sportsmen who years ago would never have faced anything more rugged than a quail hunt or fishing trip after black bass near home find themselves taking off on high-country mule deer and elk hunts, flying to northern Canada after Arctic char, plunging into the bush on a bear hunt, or following hounds on a lion chase in southwestern desert mountains. Opportunities are almost endless and a great many persons in average circumstances can and do avail themselves of them.

This means that every year thousands are planning what to them will be new adventures. They will be thrusting themselves into outdoor situations with which they are wholly unfamiliar, getting involved in strange terrains. It seems to me therefore that all sportsmen should have a fundamental knowledge of what general *areas* of this continent and what *waters* are most likely to lead them into emergency situations. Relate this information to the various *species* of fish, game birds and game animals you will pursue. Because fish and game occupy the same habitats that outdoorsmen other than hunters and fishermen also visit, much material relating to the species will be just as valid for the non-sportsman.

Fishing Hazards

We might begin with *fish*, chiefly because most sportsmen seldom consider that fish as well as big-game animals can lead them into trouble.

Black bass. The largemouth bass and its relative the smallmouth are the most popular freshwater sport fishes in the U.S. Odd as it may seem, their changing habitats over past years have gotten a good many anglers with boats into serious trouble.

Bass have been transplanted to the extent that their range today is nationwide. The construction of hundreds of large dams, forming impoundments of huge size, has progressed at such a pace that there is more surface acreage in these than in natural lakes. Today they are the foremost black bass waters.

Use caution on large, open lakes where stiff, unbroken winds can create extremely dangerous conditions for small craft.

The major share of these impoundments are scattered throughout the Mid-South, the Deep South, the Midwest, the Plains states and Texas. However, others now are found in such diverse locations as Oregon (Owyhee is an example), and Arizona-Utah-Nevada (Lake Mead, Lake Powell, Mojave, Havasu). To the unwary or incautious, these large manmade lakes can be very dangerous waters. Each extends across tens of thousands of surface acres, and commonly shorelines are hundreds of miles long. The danger for fishermen is rough water.

Consider that many of these lakes allow a stiff wind from a certain direction an uninterrupted path of fifty to one hundred miles straight up. I have seen such bass-renowned lakes as Falcon, on the lower Rio Grande, when a hard wind blowing for a couple of days made them literally too dangerous for anything less than a seaworthy cruiser of thirty to thirty-six feet. They are often more dangerous than open ocean expanses. Numerous bass fishermen and pleasure boaters have drowned in large impoundments simply because they badly underestimated them.

Strict adherence to all Coast Guard and state regulations is the first preventive. Having someone on shore know the general part of the lake where you'll be is next. And don't switch plans! Attention to storm warnings is mandatory. But if you are out on such a lake when a storm comes up, and you may be many miles from dock, unless you are positively equipped to ride it home, make for a protected cove immediately. Most impoundments have many, because flooding filled numerous small valleys and canyons. There are hundreds of spots where you can tie up, or get your light skiff ashore. Stay put, even if you have to stay overnight.

If you have an accident that disables your craft and you can get it to shore, again, stay right there. And relax. You will be found. Occasionally you may be near a marina or a dwelling and can get to a telephone. But on scores of the larger impoundments there are immense stretches of true or near wilderness areas along the shores, often in mountainous locales. Walking out can be rougher than you think and can lead to very serious consequences, for example in the deserts around such enormous expanses as Utah-Arizona's Lake Powell, or in the deep forests surrounding such a lake as the 182,000-acre Toledo Bend on the Texas-Louisiana line. "Stay with your boat" is the best advice you can get. And I repeat, have someone ashore know the general area where you are operating that day.

Dangerous situations may also arise in large swamps, such as the Everglades, where there is excellent bass fishing, or in a place like Okefenokee in southeast Georgia and across the line into Florida. Usually you will be guided in such places. By all means engage a

If your boat is disabled, find a protected area as quickly as possible and stay with your boat.

Beware of soft, slippery shorelines. Don't go wading unless you've checked to see that the bottom is firm.

guide. You can get hopelessly lost in these swamps, and even with a compass you'd be in bad trouble.

The last bass fishing warning concerns wading fishermen. Avoid soft shorelines. I once came close to losing my life while wading a lake shoreline in Michigan's Upper Peninsula. An old sawmill had been there years before. Some forty feet of decayed sawdust was under me and I was slipping and sliding on scattered slab cuttings atop it! As a rule, where such vegetation as lily pads grows, the bottom is very soft and may be treacherous. Where slender reeds grow, it is usually sandy or full of fine gravel, and firm.

Panfish, walleyes, pike, muskellunge. Most panfish are caught in quiet, smaller waters. However, white bass are schooling fish of the large impoundments and to a wide extent so are crappies. In those habitats the same cautions apply to them as to bass. Ditto for walleyes, pike, muskies, except that there are further hazards with these. Overall, the best of fishing for them is in Canada. This very often means fly-in trips, or pack-ins by various means, to backbush lakes. Don't go on these trips, guided or on your own, without maps and compass (see Chapter 5) and proper survival equipment, which will be covered in a later chapter.

Salmon, trout, grayling. Fishing for these handsome and most appealing fishes often leads to emergencies. Trips for Pacific salmon are not as likely to get you into trouble, because in most instances anglers are guided and fish from charter boats with reliable captains. Small craft occasionally get into serious trouble with these fish, however, for they venture offshore along the Pacific Coast in waters their craft are unsuited for. This is utterly foolhardy. Even if you ride the waves offshore, a blow can claim your life when you try to come in, on rocks or turbulent bars. Anglers unfamiliar with such big waters too often have too much confidence in their craft, which may have performed well in puny three-foot waves. Go on a charter boat!

Atlantic salmon are restricted in range and most of the good water is in eastern Canada. In far north-eastern Canada you are certain to be guided and must fly in. Don't go without survival gear, compass and maps. But beware of another danger with these fish: A friend of mine barely made it several seasons back when he slipped in a Gaspé salmon stream and was carried downstream a hundred yards. An inflatable fishing vest is mandatory, and waders should be belted snugly to hold air and give buoyancy. Because of slippery rocks, an absolute must is felt-soled waders.

The Rocky Mountain region, much of Canada, and portions of Maine contain the best fishing for all trout species. Inflatable vests, easy to obtain nowadays, or the foam-type jackets that give both warmth and flotation, should be mandatory for all large-stream trout fishing. A great many western streams, even some called "creeks" there, are large rivers. They can be exceeding dangerous to inept waders, first-timers, and occasionally to incautious old hands. The power of current in such rivers—perhaps the famed Madison in and outside Yellowstone Park is the best known—is difficult for the inexperienced trout fisherman to imagine. A wading staff with thong attached for securing to shoulder or belt is also an excellent help. Some are collapsible. I am skittish of these; they could let you down.

Most important on all western streams, and in many across Canada and in the Northeast, are again waders with heavy felt attached to the soles. You may locate in some stores a felt-soled buckle-on item that attaches over the foot of regular waders. There are also heavy aluminum or steel cleats that buckle over boot feet with straps. Both types keep you from slipping on slick rocks. Felt is most popular, easiest to obtain, probably best. You can even apply it yourself.

Rocks in many streams are unbelievably slippery. Drowning is not the only danger. A fall in current means your head may strike a rock. In rivers like the Gallatin south of Bozeman, Montana, and many others, where there are large boulders both above and below water, this is a serious possibility.

The other emergencies that may occur when fishing for trout, and for grayling, which are usually in remote waters, are getting lost, or having to come out from pack-ins or fly-ins. The enormous National Forests (and some BLM lands) of the West contain the lion's share of the prime U.S. trout fishing. Wilderness portions of Canada furnish a comparable amount. And of course portions of upper New England, such as the wilderness of northern Maine, and areas of the Great Lakes States like Michigan's Upper Peninsula, all are the same. Material in later chapters refers to travel in such large forest expanses.

There is one more caution relating to salmon and trout. Today the coho and the Chinook have been stocked, as many readers know, in the Great Lakes. The lake trout is also making a comeback there after near extinction by the lamprey. The emergence of the transplanted salmons as fantastic sport fish in the Great Lakes has drawn thousands of fishermen who have never before handled a boat on waters of these proportions. The Great Lakes are among the most dangerous and unpredictable of all U.S. waters. A couple of years ago a number of salmon fishermen lost their lives and scores of boats were smashed simply because anglers were not well enough equipped or well enough schooled in boat handling. The potential for trouble is still there. Treat the Great Lakes with awe and respect, obey official warnings, and outfit properly. Nobody can tell you in a book how to get out of trouble in a Great Lakes storm you have underestimated. You probably won't! Best advice is to avoid it!

Beaches. There are not many lonely coasts left along our marine beaches where fishermen can lose themselves. Basic emergencies among saltwater fishermen come chiefly from three sources: using craft too small for bluewater operation; carelessness or lack of knowledge about currents and undertows when wade-fishing the surf; accidents from slipping on wet, algae-covered jetties.

About the first there is little that can be said. We can only caution boatmen against venturing into big water with small boats. Regarding the dangers of wading surf and rips, beginners should avoid getting in much past their knees, and should take the advice of, and observe, old hands past that depth. Accidents on rock jetties and other slippery surfaces have been more commonplace than most believe. The result is not nice to

Don't let yourself get knocked off balance in wading surfs and rips. To be safe, wear steel cleats or ice creepers over your footgear, and, beginners especially, avoid deep water.

describe. There are two rules: Whenever you walk on such places, wear steel cleats or regulation ice creepers over your foot gear; when wind and waves are high, stay off!

There are a few beaches where vehicle breakdowns or exhaustion might get you into trouble. The longest stretch of uninhabited marine beach in the U.S. now is the Padre Island National Seashore on the Texas coast. The island is about 115 miles long, the Seashore roughly 88 miles long. A dredged cut across the Island about halfway stops explorers from either end. It is deep and can be treacherous on moving tides. There are three rules for people in trouble on Padre or any comparable beach: Be sure someone knows where you are going and when you planned to return; in hot weather, rig whatever shelter you can for shade; stay put. Coast Guard or Park Service personnel will find you in short order.

Birds and Animals

The roster of game birds and animals undoubtedly lures more sportsmen into emergencies than do fish. Surprising as it may seem, game birds cause hunters a lot of trouble. Part of it stems from the fact that wing-shooting seems innocuous and generally tied to well-settled locales. This should not lull the hunter. He should recognize the several potential dangers and know what to do about them.

Waterfowl. Of the birds tied to marsh and water habitats, geese, which feed chiefly in open fields, are the only ones that seldom mean trouble. Ducks and rails, in both freshwater and saltwater marshes, are the troublemakers.

Rails are hunted chiefly along the large salt marshes of the East Coast and the upper Gulf Coast, by two methods: wading and slogging muddy areas where deep canals may have to be forded, and by hunting from a boat with a guide poling the marshes. Invariably trouble can be laid to tides. If you walk, be sure you know tide times. You may be trapped and unable to get back to high ground. In a boat, there are occasions when a light craft can be pulled over a mud flat safely either to or from the hunting grounds. Hunting is always on the high tides, which push birds out of hiding. The safety rule here is absolutely never to leave your boat. If the bottom is especially soft, take no chances. Stay in the boat and suffer until tide change!

There are a few large marshes, especially along the upper Gulf Coast, where a duck hunter can easily become lost. When hunting such spots, map and compass are just as important as in wilderness big-game hunting. More so because there are so few major landmarks. Marsh-wading duck hunters also get into trouble. Soft spots can let you down so deep, in such thick, sucking mud that you cannot get out. You should realize that getting stuck collapses boots or waders against the legs so severely that you cannot pull your legs out of the boot as a desperate measure. Don't wade marshes you're unfamiliar with, unless you have checked with local experienced hunters about marsh conditions. Be especially wary of wading across open cuts and channels. A hard wind may lower water in these and make them wadeable, but the mud may be a dozen feet deep on bottom and once you go down, that's all. A few years ago this actually happened to a young duck hunter near Detroit, Michigan. By great good fortune he was rescued before the wind laid and water poured back in. But it took several men to extricate him.

The rule for waterfowlers hunting from boats is never to leave the boats behind. If lowering water along a seacoast puts the boat out of commission on a mudflat, stay in it until help comes or the water rises. If you have motor trouble, or some other difficulty, stay with the boat. If you have left word where you are going and about when you hope to return, you'll be found quickly. Trying to slog ashore may court disaster.

Pheasants, Huns, quail. Farmland game birds such as pheasants, Huns, bobwhite quail are not likely to lead you into survival situations. Desert quail, such as scaled, Gambel's, and California, might, and bobwhites might in certain regions. Desert quail, and bobwhites in the South, place a hunter in the areas of greatest concentrations of rattlesnakes. A bit about this will be found in a later chapter. But right here is a good place to note that snake leggings—aluminum or wire net with canvas covering—are readily available and provide excellent insurance.

The desert quail in the Southwest and West can lure a dedicated wingshot into losing himself, for they are great runners. Here again, map and compass are never amiss, and some knowledge of desert survival (see later chapter) is important. These quail are often found in huge expanses of arid and sparsely populated range. Don't let them beckon you into trouble when you had intended to go "just a few steps" from the vehicle!

Grouse. Getting lost does not require a vast expanse of solid woods. Remember that well! Scores of ruffed grouse hunters lose themselves by seeing a bird cross a backwoods trail, parking their cars and going after it. A hunter strange to dense woods may not believe that he can be no more than fifty yards in and yet not be able to look back and spot his vehicle.

The reason I emphasize ruffed grouse is that it is widespread, from the large forests of New England south into the rugged mountains of western North Carolina and west throughout much of the Rockies and the Pacific slopes. It draws a lot of hunters. Material in later chapters relative to map, compass, equipment is all pertinent and I strongly advise that ruffed grouse hunters and woodcock hunters (woodcock are found in the same coverts) take along basic survival gear in a small rucksack, even on "short" jaunts.

The mountain grouse, such as blue, spruce, and ptarmigan (presently legal in Colorado and perhaps soon in Washington), are wilderness birds that require the same "travel instructions" as the big game of the Rockies and Canada. The U.S. National Forests and the public forest lands of Canada are where most huntters will encounter these birds. These are large expanses where emergencies are common.

The prairie grouse—sage grouse, prairie chicken, sharptail—are not likely to lose anybody, except in a very few instances where sharptails are found in large burns and scrub willow regions of Canada. Seldom will hunters purposely hunt these birds there, but you may take them as incidentals (also true of spruce and blue grouse) while hunting big game. Invariably you will, by law, have to be guided. Prairie grouse hunters within the U.S. should heed one caution: Sage grouse, and occasionally sharptails, are often hunted in early fall or late summer, and rattlesnake danger in their habitats is fairly high.

Chukar partridge. This introduced bird is now avidly hunted in a number of western states. It may be found in reasonably civilized regions. But not often. Its prime range is in some very tough expanses of rocky ridges and cheatgrass slopes far removed from settlement. The chukar is a runner, invariably uphill. It can lose its pursuers on occasion, and chukar hunters can easily get into injury or vehicle-breakdown difficulties.

Small game. Rabbits and squirrels seldom get outdoorsmen into trouble. But two varieties can. One is the snowshoe hare (rabbit) of northern cedar swamps and mountains, from Maine to Washington, most avidly hunted in forested portions of New England and the Great Lakes in winter. It dwells in winter within dense cover such as cedar and alder swamps. These are real "man losers," and at a bad time of year. If you get into trouble in snow, backtrack; don't flounder onward.

The other species is the gray squirrel, a forest squirrel found in greatest abundance throughout the Ozarks, southern and mid-south forests, and in lesser abundance farther north. National and State Forests and similar large woodland expanses, often of dense big

You can lose yourself easily by chasing after gray squirrel in heavily forested areas. Have map and compass along for protection.

timber like oak, provide the chief hunting ground. Gray squirrel trouble has caught up with a number of hunters because they couldn't imagine a "little ole cat squirrel" being dangerous. Map and compass are good protection.

Big game. Antelope on the plains are not likely to lose anyone. But they can cause minor difficulties through vehicle breakdowns. Much depends on the state where you hunt. In New Mexico, for example, hunts are so thoroughly policed by game wardens that help is probably close by. In large expanses of Montana or Wyoming you might be a good many open-country miles from assistance. However, any nonresident hunter anywhere is usually being guided. Watch out for rattlesnakes. Stalking antelope hunters have been bitten.

Mountain sheep, mountain goats, the large northern bears, caribou and moose are wilderness creatures. But in nearly every state and province a guide must be retained in order to hunt them. Certainly there is less danger of emergencies when one is guided. The sheep and goats especially get hunters into injury situations, because of the necessity of climbing. All wilderness travel precautions apply when hunting any one of the above.

Elk are high-country animals hunted throughout much of the Rocky Mountain region. They are exceedingly wild, likely to travel long distances. A wounded elk can lead a hunter many miles. Fortunately most elk live in high mountain terrain where landmarks are numerous, even though settlement is sparse. The western National Forests are prime elk terrain. A major share of hunts are guided, or a group of hunters operates together. Injury, breakdown, fall snowstorms, getting lost are all hazards of elk country. Again, proper equipment and knowledge are mandatory.

Black bears are a prize many hunters eagerly seek. Bears are chased by hounds owned by guides, or they are baited in spring. In most bait hunts, the hunter is guided, stays by his stand, and is later picked up. Certainly if you walk in, in strange territory, you should have map and compass and other moderate equipment. Anyone who deliberately sets out to follow a black bear track—and this happens as well to deer and elk hunters in fall—is not only a bit foolhardy but generally wasting his time. Black bears ramble aimlessly, and many miles. Throughout their range, which covers most of the forested regions of the U.S. and Canada, they favor dense cover where the going for a man is rough. Black bear hunters should carry survival gear.

Deer. Of all the lost men and all the hunters injured each season in the woods, snowed in, broken down, and bogged down, deer, whitetails and mule deer, are responsible for most of the difficulty. In today's world many animals live on the fringes of civilization. They have adapted well. This is especially true of whitetails, abundant over almost all of the U.S. east of the Mississippi and in certain regions west of it, such as Texas, the Plains states, the east slope of the Rockies and isolated pockets elsewhere. But by and large the several million deer hunters operate in the State and National Forests, border to border and coast to coast. And in any area under forest conditions, and under mountain-forest conditions for mule deer of the West, you always run the risk of emergency.

Most deer hunters get into trouble, often serious trouble, through plain carelessness. Portions of what is to be said here apply to all other hunting or fishing endeavors.

First, a major share of deer hunters go out "just for the day," that is, a single day at a time, in territory they know, or think they know, rather well. But somehow they get turned around or they wound a deer and follow it, or they decide at the last minute to hunt in a different place than originally intended. These one-day-at-a-time hunters, even on their home grounds if not in a farmland community, should be equipped with map and compass and basic survival gear. Someone should know precisely the area where the day's hunt is to be done, and the hunter should never deviate from his set plan.

Second, thousands of deer hunters camp out in the forests, usually in groups. A vast amount of trouble oc-

Taking off suddenly on a short hunt near camp is a foolhardy idea. With no survival equipment except a gun, and no one knowing where you intended to go, there won't be much help if you meet with trouble.

curs because certain hunters set out for just a quick little turn in the woods near camp, and are found three days later in bad shape some miles away. The "short hunt near camp" (or vehicle) is one of the worst troublemakers, because invariably the hunter sets off without any equipment except his gun. Commonly he doesn't even take a jacket, or matches. He wounds a deer, or is lured on and on by flying grouse, and shortly he is lost and without survival equipment. No one knows where to look.

Remember once again that you *always* set out, even on short jaunts, as if you really planned to get lost or get into some kind of trouble. Deer hunters, because they are so numerous and because so many are really inexperienced, hunting only a few days a season, should especially heed this advice. Be sure someone knows where you are going, and always go prepared for emergency.

Wounded game. There are two more items that should be noted here. Each season a number of hunters are injured by wounded game. Usually they are alone, probably not expected back for some hours, and thus in serious trouble. I knew a deer hunter who shot his first deer, raced to it, set his gun against a tree, started to gut the deer. It leaped up, knocked him down, broke his leg, and escaped.

There are endless variations. A "dead" bear kills a hunter, a downed moose tosses its head and injures the carelessly eager trophy taker. Be positive a downed animal is dead. Move in slowly, gun ready. Never under any circumstances set the gun down until you are positive. Never have it slung over a shoulder. A big buck mule deer almost got me head-on a few years ago as I paced off the distance of my shot, walking with gun slung. The deer came off the ground in a vicious lunge when I was just seven paces away. It fell. If it had not, certainly I could not have stopped the charge. A method suggested by some hunters is to cautiously approach the downed animal and, even though you're certain it is dead, touch its eye with the end of the gun barrel.

A number of injuries occur because a supposedly dead antlered animal jerks its head reflexively while a hunter attempts to move it for gutting or actually starts to gut it. Antlers can be very dangerous. Stay shy of them. Even when you're trying to move for gutting or draining a gutted big-game animal that is "for sure" dead, be cautious of getting hurt by the antlers.

The final item of importance is to be cautious with your knife. A few years ago a well-known outdoor writer nearly died from blood loss when he accidentally slashed his leg gutting a mule deer. A hunter is usually excited from the kill when he starts the gutting process. He is usually hurrying, impatient. Make it a rule, however, to take your time and to keep foremost in your mind that an emergency could be shaping up to ruin an otherwise enjoyable hunt!

4 / *What You Need for Emergencies*

Not long ago I met a young outfitter who used a cheap, skinny sleeping bag, no mattress, and just flopped. He sure went light, and he sure was young and tough, but he also got up lame, hurt almost every day, and caught cold incessantly. Meanwhile, I broke out my down pillow, the same one I use at home, crawled into my wonderful big bag, and slept on foam plastic three inches thick. The pack mule, I can assure you, never thought twice about those packages. It would have kicked just as hard if it hadn't carried anything.

I believe in being rested and as comfortable as I can get, when I am going, and there and everything is perking along okay. However, when an emergency crops

up, things change. At such times you must have
squirreled away the items that will do best for you
under specific and sometimes lean circumstances.

Survival and Comfort

This is when *comfort* can go hang. You must have
available all of the items necessary to your *safety,* but
not necessarily to your *full comfort.* My two themes
are not incongruous. For example, there are many
sleeping bags that can be placed one inside the other.
The result is a delightful, full-comfort sleeping arrangement when all goes well. But by stripping down you
can get out of an emergency light and alive. That big
foam mattress is great, but I could turn my back on it
in emergency because I have already prepared some
sort of groundcloth or other piece of basic equipment,
to make do if and when dire need arises.

We are talking about a two-in-one outfit in some far-
back situations. I want comfort. But I don't believe
that in an emergency it is worth even a passing thought.
Survival and *comfort,* as modern outdoorsmen know
them, are not companions.

A history of early voyageurs on the Red River of the
North related how men had to line boats up the river
in bitter weather. Even the toughest became ill at times.
The diarist recorded: "We had two sick men with fever.
But the captain said that unless they were dead in
three days they were well. One died. The other two re-
covered, but had to continue to wade and labor in the
bitter water and weather."

The ability to suffer gracefully, or at least stoically,

is one great asset for the man in emergency. Here again mental control is crucial. Bear with it. Nobody else is going to sympathize with you! The word "survival" means getting back alive. It has no relation to wallowing in lush creature comforts and having a delightful time.

Survival Pack

Your pack for survival in any situation, therefore, is based on the most basic *attempts* at comfort. Maid service is out. What you want are the fundamentals, in as compact and light a conglomeration of gear as you can fit to the situation.

The first and most important "equipment" to take with you is the knowledge that someone outside knows where you are headed, how long you are to stay, and by what route and when you are returning. That is the easiest, probably the most important, and most often overlooked part!

What you are doing, how long you intend to be gone, how remote the territory, and your mode of transport dictates your choice of emergency kit or pack or equipment from there on. The average outdoorsman who is going fishing on a large lake, for a one-day canoe trip, into the woods after grouse, on a morning deer hunt, or hiking to a trout stream for a day should have a small rucksack that is constantly packed and ready. It need not be very heavy. It can contain scores of small items, or a very few that will be handy for comfort or necessary in emergency.

Start with this basic small pack. It can be a Boy Scout

type packsack, or a larger or even a smaller one. Most of the items to be placed in it, remember, are ones that will be needed on more extended jaunts, too. So all you have to do is think carefully about the vital items. What does *any animal* including the human need for contentment? Food, water, safety, comfort. There are varying degrees of all four. Basically the human animal needs to be able to build a fire under any weather conditions, keep reasonably dry, reasonably warm, sleep if necessary in relative comfort, eat, and quench thirst.

First Aid Kit

First of all should come a first aid kit. There are widely varying opinions as to what this should contain. There are some very good pamphlets and booklets on first aid. There are scores of excellent first-aid kits already made up and sold in drugstores. Most good ones contain a small instruction manual, and a snakebite kit. Seldom will the snakebite kit have antivenin, however, so in snake country you must add that.

In addition, there should be a supply of band-aid plastic strips, plus butterfly-type closures for larger cuts. Gauze pads, thick ones about 4 inches square, possibly a half dozen of them, are needed for wound dressing. Wide elastic bandage, a roll of plastic adhesive, not the older cloth type, safety pins, small soap bar—these are the basics, plus merthiolate, aspirin, a tube of first-aid cream, another of burn ointment, and one or two of the modern small plastic squirt bottles for treatment of insect bites and stings. The merthiolate or comparable medicines should be replaced at intervals so they

An effective first aid kit that weighs only a few ounces includes several first aid creams, soap, merthiolate and aspirin, a variety of bandages and adhesive, safety pins, Q-tips, and snakebite kit with antivenin. In closed, waterproof bags carry a few clean handkerchiefs and a first aid instruction booklet.

do not get too old. In some latitudes sunburn cream (not oil that may spill) should be included.

Check out the various "sportsman's first aid kits" in stores and see what each contains. Some come in water-proof containers. Add a couple of clean handkerchiefs in a small, closed plastic bag. And be sure to have in your pack, not necessarily as a part of a first-aid kit, a small squeeze bottle or two of the new and highly potent cream-type insect repellent. This first-aid kit will weigh only a few ounces. You may wish to vary it somewhat, but the above should serve as a guide.

Survival Clothing

It is difficult to suggest clothing for a small pack, because of the great range of temperatures where outdoorsmen may be. However, I made a rule long ago that regardless of what part of the country I was in, I'd always have a down jacket with me. I've seen days in Texas when the temperature dropped from 90 to 40 in a few hours. I've seen the same in Canada, and the Rockies of the U.S. West. The light jacket half of a down underwear suit is the best I know about. Worn under a wool shirt, and with a nylon outer windbreaker, you can stay warm with it in vicious weather. It can also serve, rolled up, as a pillow when not needed for warmth.

Particularly for fall, I squeeze into a small packet a down underwear jacket, if I'm not wearing it. Let me digress here to say that on long hauls, where a large pack is made up, possibly to be carried on horseback, you should take along the full down underwear suit. It's light, can be compressed into a small space. Worn inside a light backpacker sleeping bag, the combo is like a double bag.

For the small pack we're talking about, the next clothing item is one of those little nylon windbreakers mentioned above—in red or orange or blaze orange.

Not yellow. That color can be confused with aspen or other abundant leaves in fall. Blaze orange is best. In the pack also is a rain suit of waterproofed nylon, pants and parka. If you are on horseback, you'll have a poncho tied behind your saddle. That's standard. But ponchos are heavy. The *quality* nylon rain suit is very light and packs into a small space.

In summer you may wish to delete one or another of these clothing items. But as a guide to comfort in almost any sort of emergency, these are the fundamentals.

A spare pair of warm gloves or mittens, and a spare pair of socks suitable for hiking should always be in your pack. For long trips, two pairs of socks. Also, I have long puzzled over why so few outdoorsmen who wear leather boots fail to purchase waterproof brands. There are several on the market, excellent quality, perfect for comfort, and literally waterproof. Insulated boots, incidentally, are fine even for fairly warm weather. They are also less wearing on your feet.

A notation here pertaining to water-related clothing and life-saving devices: In an earlier chapter I mentioned that fishermen wading large rivers should wear inflatable fishing vests. There are a number of these available. This is an important item for the pack of any fisherman, whether he will wade or fish from a boat or canoe. But of course he should wear it when on the water.

Another excellent product nowadays is a jacket that is worn comfortably in any hunting, fishing, or other outdoor activity, but that floats you like a life preserver if the need arises. These jackets are usually nylon on the exterior, with insulation that has thousands of built-in air cells. One of the better quality brands was tested not long ago, and after repeated immersions it still floated a man weighing over 200 pounds while he was wearing chest-high waders filled with water. These jackets can be compressed into a small space for packing, are light and very warm. For the waterfowl hunter or fisherman, this is a good choice for land-water combo wear. In addition to the above, the well known pocket-size Res-Q-Pak, the little emergency life preserver that inflates by CO_2 when squeezed, should be a part of every pack, large or small. It does no harm to have two. But be sure not to forget to wear it on the water.

Special Items

Needless to say your compass and map are packed, along with a pencil for drawing necessary map lines. A small flashlight with fresh batteries is a good idea to add, plus extra batteries if there's room. I always carry, even on one-day jaunts, a few of those small paper packets of salt that restaurants or drive-ins often use. These are wrapped in plastic or placed in a small waterproof plastic container. A good knife is a must. This can be a knife worn on the belt, or a folding knife. It is a good idea to wear your belt knife but to keep a spare, a good folding knife, in your pack. There are numerous odds and ends that may come in handy: a few long leather shoe laces, for lashings in making a shelter; a spool of *heavy* fishing line; a roll of copper wire.

For emergency shelter, there are two items that can be packed in surprisingly small space compared to the amount of comfort they supply. One is a rubberized or plastic-coated nylon ground sheet or tarp. This should be about 8 x 8 feet. It folds flat in the bottom of your packsack. The other is a large sheet of heavy plastic. I have a friend who has been an innovator in winter camping. He has taken groups over the Continental

The miscellaneous section of your pack is as essential as the rest. A rubberized tarp and leather shoelaces provide emergency shelter; a good knife, rolls of heavy fishing line and copper wire, and salt packets in a waterproof container cover food possibilities. Other necessary items are a pencil, map and compass, and a flashlight with fresh and extra batteries.

Divide in dead of winter with sleeping gear consisting of a backpack sleeping bag and a big sheet of heavy plastic. They simply lay the sheet on snow, place the bag on it, wrap the plastic around and tuck it in. Such a sheet can also be used to make a lean-to or other type of shelter. The lashing material is used with either plastic or nylon tarp.

Fire Equipment

Now to emergency fire-making equipment. You must carry matches in a completely moisture-proof container. There are several types available. Shy away from metal. It rusts and may be hard to open with cold hands. Large kitchen matches are the only kind to take. Squirrel away plenty of them. Paper matches are useless, small wooden matches not much better. But that's not the end of the fire-making apparatus.

Fire is so important that there is a full chapter devoted to it later on. But to keep items for emergency all together here, I must add that I believe in being over-prepared with the basics for fire-making. For example, there are numerous solid-state fire-starter materials on the market. A small box of these is invaluable for damp or windy conditions, especially since most persons who will really need a fire probably won't be too adept at building one under any but optimum campground conditions.

There is also the Metal Match. I believe that is a trade name, and though it is not our intent to plug brand names here, I don't happen to know of any other. The Ute Mountain Corporation in Denver is at this time the outlet for these. They really work. And, you can get a kit that contains ready-made tinder to catch the sparks. This outfit takes up such a tiny corner that I would not be without it, in addition to matches. And this brings up the fact that most fire-making instructions tell you how to collect punk or highly inflammable materials around you, from the woods. Fine. But better still, *have it ready,* in your pack, in the small packet with the fire-starter cubes.

Now add a magnifying glass about 3 inches in diameter. Though a camera lens or binocular lens or even a watch crystal may start a fire, the small glass can stay permanently in your pack. Hold it so sun shining through it focuses a small "hot spot" on the tinder or starter you already have. This glass serves a double purpose. I have spent a great deal of time in desert areas where cactus and thornbrush are abundant and can always use the small glass, and a *pair of good tweezers.* Both can be packed in your first-aid kit. The glass doubles for fire-making if needed. The tweezers remove those tiny cactus (or other) spines the glass "sees" that make life miserable but can't be removed with your nails or a knife point. Always stow in your pack, whether it is large or small, several candles. They should be those short, fat ones often called "plumbers' candles."

If you will review these odds and ends, you will discover you have fire-making equipment for almost any conceivable condition. If tinder is wet, dry it with the candle flame. You are outfitted to stay dry and warm. Even on one-day jaunts, if you take the down underwear jacket, you can sleep out with no bag in fair comfort.

Food and Water

For short jaunts, or what are intended to be short ones, you cannot carry everything. I would not bother

with a mess kit. It is easy to cook fish, or birds, or
frogs, etc., on sticks over an open fire. But for long
trips I certainly would have a light, basic-item mess
kit in a pack: a container in which to boil water, another to cook in, a spoon. A packet of heavy foil, folded
flat, has endless uses in cooking.

Halazone tablets should be in a pack, for purifying
water. There are also compact water-purifying kits of
several kinds, even battery-powered, on the market.
Check any one of these with care before buying, however, to be positive it works as it should. On any warm-
weather journey, even brief, a canteen of water is mandatory. You know best how much you require. For
desert travel never be without a sizable canteen. I have
convinced several friends to carry in addition an ordinary pint liquor flask full of water, for emergency use.

This leaves only food. A lot of living off the country,
which we will discuss later on, can be done. But even
on those short treks it is wise to have a small store of
emergency grub. The amount must be matched to the
terrain and its hazards. With foil and lightweight packets of freeze-dried or concentrated foods, excellent
emergency meals are at hand. Wild foods supplement
them. Numerous freeze-dried and concentrated foods
are readily available nowadays.

A food that is to my knowledge not available com-
mercially today, but a topnotch one we have made
several times, is pemmican. I presume ours didn't taste
just like old-fashioned Indian pemmican. But it keeps
as theirs did, indefinitely, and it has all the emergency
ingredients you need for days at a time. On many a
day's hunt I have stowed a hunk of this, wrapped in

foil, in my light packsack and used it and nothing else for lunch. Obviously you cannot carry great quantities of food on short journeys in a light pack. A tin or two of sardines, cocoa, raisins, nuts—these are suggestions. I would advise sportsmen such as deer hunters to *always* have along enough to "make do" for a day or so just in case.

Now then, all of the foregoing can be carried in a light packsack on short trips. At that, it may not be so light if you take along every item mentioned. But you can pick and choose according to where you are, where you are going, and balance the gear against the chances of emergency. You can make up a pack that will weigh no more than five pounds, and up to ten, that will allow you to live virtually "free and wild" in modest weather for weeks at a time, if you add to it a bit of ingenuity.

Long Trips

For longer trips, such as by horse or plane or 4WD, some extra equipment is needed. As you select these items, think about how you can relate them to *what you will be using anyway*. In other words, this does not need to be all extra gear. It can serve both purposes. For example, you can make up a backpack outfit, an ultra-light quality one, that contains a tent of three or four pounds and a sleeping bag of like weight. By combining down underwear, as noted, with such a bag, you can get along well on any sort of trip. This outfit should be on a light packframe. It can be lashed this way, all packed, on a pack animal. It should also contain basic cooking utensils, and items previously mentioned.

Wonderfully planned backpack outfits are available nowadays, designed by people who practice the sport of backpacking weeks at a time. Check the literature on these, or look them over in stores, and figure which size will be best for you. Then if you get into a situation where you have to walk out, you are ready to go. Don't stint too much on weight. A properly put together and balanced pack of thirty-five pounds is not bad, and it will let you tote most of the ingredients for safety, shelter, warmth and food. You can cut that by ten pounds and still have a good emergency outfit.

Gaff hook and wire. There are some other things that might be considered. A good many years ago I was sent by a magazine to do an undercover story about some natives in Canada who had a hobby of illegally gaffing big trout during their spring spawning runs. I hiked with these people many miles into the bush, to a small stream running into Lake Superior. I had no idea of how the man heading the expedition intended to accomplish their mission. He carried a canvas pack on his back, but I saw no evidence of gaff or spear.

When we were at destination, he cut some stout, straight sticks about an inch in diameter and six feet long. He notched one end with a groove several inches long, and a cross groove in two spots. Now he hauled from his packsack several gaff hooks. Just the hook part and several inches of shaft that was flattened on the upper end. Next, out came a roll of copper wire. He lashed the gaffs to the sticks. These were used to strike big trout as they dashed up or down stream. These men were expert at it. One would make a pass at a four-pounder, the gaff would nail it, and in one motion the poacher threw gaff and all onto the bank.

I have often thought that this combo, gaff hook and wire, might come in handy in an emergency. I've never had to try, but have carried one several times. It is a good item in a pack for the far-back trip, especially during seasons when fish may be running in streams. But it could be used at other times by a careful stalker.

Binoculars. I never go anywhere in the forest, on horseback or otherwise, without a binocular. It has many uses besides hunting. It is a good emergency item for scanning country, seeking landmarks to get yourself oriented. I wear mine, but not flopping as most do. Shorten the strap so the glass lies fairly high on your chest. Make up a couple of tie downs (one a spare) of quarter- or half-inch elastic with hook and eye at the end, length cut to fit your chest and hold the glass snugly. You can now lift it to your eyes by stretching the elastic, let it down again where it won't flop and bounce.

Tools. Though a full-fledged camp on a pack trip will have a good axe, it would be foolish to carry one of full size for emergency gear. But a good sharp hatchet, in a sheath, carried in a pack or on your belt, is a must item. You may also find a kind of substitute in sporting goods stores, a head with blade and ripper that has a hole through it with heavy screw threads, into which you twist a cut stick for a handle. The good hatchet, all-steel handle, is probably best.

I also carry a saw. But I disagree with some others about what kind. The tiny wire-cable emergency saws aren't of much account. Nor are the so-called "pocket folding saws," the ten-inch saws that have a blade folding into the handle. These are toys. There is, however, a slightly larger saw of this folding type that is excellent. The blade is heavy duty, with coarse teeth, and curved exactly right to make a cut. It is a blade comparable to those used in long-handled tree-pruning saws. When folded, this saw, which costs only three or four dollars, is roughly fifteen inches long. I have cut trees six inches or more in diameter very easily with one. This often substitutes admirably for a hatchet, and in fact can more quickly do many chores that the hatchet does: cutting firewood or erecting shelters. Both, in a pack for long hauls, are sound equipment.

On wilderness hunting trips, fishing trips, or even simple hiking trips for neither purpose, I suggest some special compact fishing gear be a part of the pack. Nowadays you can buy a variety of what are called "backpack" rods. Strictly for survival purposes, the spinning or casting rod in this type will be best. These come broken down in small aluminum cases only 18 to 24 inches long, depending on the make. A light but sturdy line-filled reel for the chosen rod, stowed in a drawstring soft leather case is next. The line should be fairly heavy. Add an extra spool of line. In a small packet or plastic tube or box, put a few hooks of modest size, and a few split shot. Take line, hooks, and shot whether or not you take rod and reel.

In a flat snap-shut lure box, or better still a leather

or cloth zipper-closure pocket-type case, place a collection of metal spoons. These should be in several sizes, from three inches long down to three-fourths of an inch, and in varying colors. And here's the trick. Remove hooks from all. Outfit each spoon with a split ring. Numerous spoons can now be carried in a very small package. Leave the treble and double hooks at home. Take along in a small box some *single* hooks of various sizes, to place on the spoons as needed. A small pair of pointed-nose pliers fills out the outfit. The rod can be placed in the backpack, or lashed to it. The other gear takes up little space. Though you may not realize it, almost any species of fish found on the continent can be caught on spoons. If you don't take rod and reel, you can rig a brush-cut pole and make short casts with a spoon.

Firearms. A word should be said about firearms. If you are on a hunting trip, whether short or long, your survival pack should contain at least a few spare rounds of ammunition for the gun you are carrying. Many outdoorsmen nowadays have the naive idea that addition of a small sidearm will help them live off the country. Most couldn't hit the ground with it, let alone kill an animal or bird. Except for handgun experts, sidearms are more or less dude equipment. Also, you may get into trouble by shooting at large animals such as bears with it. There are small .22 rifles made that fold, or come apart easily, or that carry the barrel within the stock, etc. All these are very light, and in a pinch on a long trip by plane, boat or canoe, or even back-packing, it might be handy to have one in the pack. This is up to you.

Of great importance are signaling devices. Signaling is so important that a chapter is devoted to it later on. But to keep pack item ideas together, a few suggestions follow. These can go into the small short-hike rucksack as well as into large packs. A whistle is one, the kind that can be heard long distances. A signaling mirror is another. This is not an ordinary mirror but one designed purposely for signaling. (See chapter on Signaling.) These are generally available at such places as marine supply stores. Flares are available in a very small package that also contains the small gun for shooting them. Larger flares that burn longer are thrust into the ground. The small shooting flares are easiest to carry. Signaling smoke candles that emit yellow smoke can be obtained, too.

Try to relate the suggestions given here to your needs and your usage. You can't carry everything. But you *can* balance a survival pack, large or small, to do an efficient job. That job is to allow *you to survive* with as much comfort as is possible to pack into a small space and weight. Emphasis here is on the one-day trippers even more than on the long-haulers. Horseback, boat, 4WD and plane trips are usually planned rather well by an outfitter to begin with. Most outdoorsmen get into trouble, as we said earlier, because they are "just going to step off the road for a second" or there is a deer near camp and the cook can't resist going after it, trailing it when it is wounded, and winding up getting lost with no survival gear.

So, regardless of *where* you're going—down the big impoundment in your boat, for a fifteen-minute flight to a forest landing strip, on a one-day horseback or hiking jaunt to a trout stream or lake, or plunging into the woods when you see that bird cross the road and you park your car to go after it—take your little pack along. You know what it really is? *Home!*

5 / Map and Compass

A GOOD COMPASS and a map of the region where you are operating are the two most important items to carry. This does not apply only to wilderness endeavors. Even on a pheasant or quail or cottontail hunt in a well-settled countryside strange to the hunters, or on a fishing jaunt to a new lake or stream, both are very handy. An up-to-date road map helps you find the place from which you start, or locates landmarks and in some cases woodlots or state and county forests. The compass saves time in getting to and from where you want to go. Not that you are lost or are likely to become lost during such "civilized" sessions: the compass and map are simply handy. But far more important, if you get used to never being without them, and ac-

customed to using both at such times, you will have
formed a habit that may save your life sometime in
the future.

A few years ago I was hunting in the Pigeon River
State Forest in northern Michigan. That Forest contains slightly less than 100,000 acres. That's around
150 square miles, and certainly ample room in which
to get lost. Nevertheless it is crisscrossed by many old
logging roads, trails and numerous streams. On the
main sand roads there are markers at intersections. Excellent county and Forest maps notwithstanding, during my days in that region numerous outdoorsmen,
both fishermen and hunters, lost themselves annually
and I am sure they still do.

It is unbelievable how many outdoorsmen carry both
map and compass, but don't know how to use either
one. They rely on a compass to "get them out." Probably the clerk who sold it couldn't have found his way
to the front door with one. And, neither map nor compass is much help if you don't know where you are to
begin with, where you started from and where you
want to get back to.

The Best Compass For You

Let us therefore start from scratch. Compass first.
There are several types. I don't intend to describe each,
but I do intend to describe one, the best one for the
average outdoorsman, tyro or expert. The extremely
simple, cheap compasses so many outdoorsmen pin on
a jacket lapel might be used advantageously in a pinch
by an expert. They more often help only in making

more confusion. The pocket-watch type is fair, but none can compare with an *orienting-type compass.*

There are several models in these. Here is a general description. This compass has a rectangular or oblong base. This base may or may not fold in the middle for compactness. In the most useful models one long and one short side of the base have ruled edges. The com-

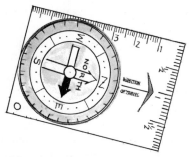

The orienting-type compass has a rectangular base and a movable housing containing the magnetic pointer. On the bottom of the transparent housing, there is a painted arrow; on the base, an arrow for sighting travel direction and ruled edges. The housing base is divided into 360°.

pass portion is affixed to the base well back toward one end, which we'll call the back end. Ahead of it there is a heavy arrow running toward the front end. This is usually an engraved, darkened arrow *to be used in sighting a travel direction.*

The compass itself is fashioned as follows: The bottom of the housing (in the models I prefer) is transparent. Across the middle of this round, transparent housing bottom there is a broad engraved, or painted, arrow. Lines run at even intervals out from this broad arrow, on either side and parallel to it. The actual compass pointer, the magnetic pointer, is affixed to this housing bottom precisely in the center of the broad arrow. The broad arrow is for orientation when you fully understand how the compass works. One end of the magnetic pointer (on the model I'm describing) is bright red. That is the end that will always point north.

Enclosing this round, transparent housing bottom and the magnetic compass pointer (needle) is the housing proper. It, too, is round, and it is also *movable*. It can be turned full circle in either direction. Its top is transparent. Around the metal edge of the top, outside the transparent disc, there are letterings: N, S, E, W. Halfway between each letter on the circle there is a heavy black line. These are read, when the compass is properly oriented, as northeast, southeast, northwest, southwest. Between each of these marks and the nearest letter there are two evenly spaced dots. These indicate gradations of an even nature, standard everywhere: NNW, which means halfway between northwest and north (sometimes read as "northwest by north"); WNW, meaning halfway between northwest and west, and so on around the circle. That is, NNE and ENE; SSE and ESE; SSW and WSW. Each of these sixteen markings—letters, lines, dots—equals a specific number of degrees when the compass is properly oriented. The marking system may differ in different brands, that is, it may have full lettering as I've given above, instead of lines and dots, but the meaning is the same.

The bottom portion of the moving, circular housing I have been describing is flanged outward and on it are numbers and lines that show *degrees* in the 360-degree circle, in 5-degree intervals. There may be deviation in design among various makes of compasses, but these are basically the parts and design of the orientation-type compass. Some of these compasses contain air, some liquid.

Taking a Reading

Lay this compass flat on your palm now, or on a table or desk or log or stump or rock outdoors to get the hang of how it works. At first, pay no attention to the position of the movable housing. Look at the magnetic arrow. If you've made certain no metal objects are near that might deflect it (in some cases a gun barrel or knife could) it will be pointing north. Now hold the base firmly with a lefthand thumb and finger, and turn the housing until the broad arrow on the housing base (the arrow that is drawn or painted or engraved on the base) is pointing in the same direction as the compass needle. This arrow and the needle should be exactly lined up, the compass needle exactly above and within the lines of the broad base arrow.

This means that the base arrow is also pointing north. Thus all of the other directions, and every degree reading along the bottom outer flange of the movable base, are now also properly aligned, pointing toward their indicated directions. This, then, is the general plane on which the compass operates.

To use the compass to plot a travel direction, line up the painted arrow in the housing with the magnetic needle. When you place the compass flat on your palm, the needle will be pointing north. Holding the base with your left hand, turn the housing until the painted arrow also points north, identically with the needle. If, for example, you want to travel west, turn the base until the letter W lines up with the direction-of-travel arrow, and set off in that direction.

However, don't forget about that big arrow engraved or otherwise marked on the compass base, the one we said was for sighting travel direction. You now know where north and thus all the other directions are. But suppose you wish to travel due west. Hold the compass base, and turn the housing until the W is lined up exactly with the direction sighting arrow. Now turn the entire compass, base and all, until the magnetic arrow and the orientation arrow below it are once again perfectly aligned. The big sighting arrow now points the way you want to go. If you were holding the compass in your hand, with the directional sighting arrow pointing straight away from you, instead of turning the compass you should turn your *body*. When the magnetic needle and the orientation arrow below it are aligned, you are actually facing exactly in the direction you intend to go. Select a landmark—a tree or rock or sharp hill—and head toward it. Never move the compass setting now as long as you wish to keep going due west, or along whatever course in degrees you have set. From that landmark, select another toward which you are pointed and your degree setting will remain the same. These are the basics of how this compass operates.

In the field it won't always be quite that simple. Suppose you head for a big rock on a distant ridge but have to cross a valley and presently can't see it. To avoid getting off course, you can sight on intermediary landmarks in between. Start perhaps with a tree in general line with the rock, but nearby. Walk to it and take a proper bearing on another, and so on, until you *can* see your target once more.

Suppose you have parked your vehicle on a road in a State Forest. You check the road with your compass. It runs due north-south. You know by your road map in the car that another road, east-west, lies a couple of miles north, and another a couple of miles south. You want to find a trout stream about a mile to the east into the woods, and you know it flows in a generally southern direction. You take a compass sighting straight East and keep checking it occasionally. If the sun is out and the time is mid-p.m. the sun will be behind you, but it will probably not be *straight* west. Its position depends upon time of year.

However, there is no difficulty finding the trout stream by compass. It is a casual project. You decide to fish wet flies, downstream, south. You fish for a couple of hours but have not yet reached another road. All you have to do is set a west course going out and you are certain, if you check often so you don't wander, to come out on the trail your car is on, and south of it. A short hike north brings you to it. Make no mistake,

> You can use a simple road map and your compass to lead you to a trout stream nearby, a short distance to the east of where you are. When you check the road with your compass, you find it runs north-south. On the map you see that another road runs east-west, a few miles to the south. With this information, you know that you must take a compass reading straight east and follow that direction to find the stream. To return to your starting point, you would merely have to hike west, until you hit the road, then north.

however. On an overcast day many a fisherman might have wandered in circles for hours in this few square miles of forest, had he not had an assist from a compass.

Rules for travel. Whether by map and compass or compass alone, there are a few rules to remember. Know where you started from: camp, car, trail intersection, lake, hill. Memorize landmarks as you travel. Keep looking *back*, so you know what to look for coming out. Mark your trail here and there if you need to, by a lopped branch or some other plainly visible marker *every thirty paces*. Look back at these markers after you've passed, to make certain they are visible on return. Always be positive that someone on the "outside" knows where you are going, and if possible the point from which you started. With an orientation-type compass as described, do not reset it when you start back. Simply point the sighting arrow on the base *toward* you instead of away. It is a good idea to jot down or memorize your degree reading in case the housing is accidentally turned.

Practice with your compass in backyard or countryside or even city walks. Try on a small-scale setting a certain course, pacing off a certain number of steps, making a right-angle setting, counting a like number of steps, another right angle turn, checked on the compass, until you have covered a square. Then try triangles. Mark the starting point. You can set a course, compass properly oriented (needle and lower arrow aligned) for any number of degrees. You go a measured (by paces) distance. Now you add 120 degrees (a third of a circle) to the first reading, if the total is not over 360 degrees. Turn either way, reorient, and set a new course. You travel the same distance, add another 120 degrees and reorient again. This third leg of like distance brings you back to your starting point. Any time your addition gets you more than 360 degrees (a circle), you subtract 360 from the total to get your reading. Such practice runs get you used to the compass and how it works, and give you confidence. It is vital to your safety, and survival, that you are "compass educated" *before* you really need its help.

Measuring Distances

Before we discuss maps, consider some facts about measuring distances. It may often be necessary to know at least fairly closely how far you have traveled or must travel. This is especially important if you are without a map, or lost. Any dedicated outdoorsman should know, and most do, the length of his *average* walking paces. Mine, on flat ground, are thirty-eight inches, two inches over a yard, from the rear heel to the forward toe. For practical purposes this means each step is a yard in average terrain. For counting, many foresters use "double paces," or the "one-two" step with the same foot each time. That would mean in my case 6 feet for each double, or a count of 880 double paces to the mile. On level ground that would be about it. Climbing or descending, rough and dense terrain will change (add to) the number somewhat. But it is still a good base figure to stow away, checked out on your own paces.

In ordinary hunting you won't be counting. But if

you are lost, you certainly had better, in order to help you know how far you have gone in any direction. Also, in locating downed game it is very handy. I killed an elk one time and had to have help getting it out. I set a compass course, counted paces to a trail, marked the spot where I emerged. Going back all we had to do was start from my mark, turn the compass around and count steps. We didn't come exactly to the animal, but by the time we were close I knew where I was and went straight to it.

In addition to counting and measuring paces, you should know how *fast* you travel. Practice, with a watch, over a known course, like half-a-mile. Try it on flat meadow or field, again climbing a rough rocky hillside, and by all means again coming down. Try it in dense brush, and in open woods. Get these figures in mind, even jotting them down in practice. Figure an all-round average. If you are going from camp to find a lake or stream, you will be trying for a straight course. Check your watch and you'll know about how far you are from camp. If you are hunting, probably you wander a lot. Still a watch check against your known general speeds will give you a good guess on how far you are from camp. Make educated guesses for terrain influence. When you are traveling a straight line with map and compass, heading for a specific point, or trying to get back to one, you will know by timing roughly how far you have gone. You'll know when you *should* have reached destination, or camp, or the vicinity. In these situations you won't be purposely wandering, as in hunting.

North and True North

All of the foregoing compass material has one serious built-in error, purposely left until now to avoid confusion. On short hikes it won't be very important, nor will it when you are going from closely visible landmark to landmark. But when you begin using *compass and map together,* on longer hauls, you will be making seriously incorrect computations, unless you understand and compensate for it. At that time it becomes urgent. You can lose yourself with your compass if you do not make the proper adjustments.

On your map, "north" means what may be termed "True North," a straight shot toward the North Pole. However, the compass needle operates magnetically and the earth's geology affects it. There are magnetic forces that upset it. Numerous magnetic lines run through the earth, from varying angles, and these converge at what may be called the "Magnetic North Pole." This is located a long distance below the True North Pole. It is located in northern Canada. It is toward this magnetic pole that the compass needle actually points.

If you happen to be at a location along one particular magnetic line, which is considered as zero, a line that runs roughly from eastern Florida up across the U.S. about to Chicago, on up through Lake Michigan and thence straight to the True North Pole, Magnetic North and True North will be the same. Your compass will be pointing at both. But if you are east or west of that line even one degree, there will be a deviation in compass reading from True North on the map. Suppose you are 10 degrees east of the line. You are aiming for a landmark a little more than half a mile distant. You make no allowance for this phenomenon, called magnetic declination. Over that half-mile-plus, you will miss your mark by about 500 feet (over 150 yards) or about 50 feet for each degree. The rule is that if you are *east* of the line, that is, you have a declination to the east, you *subtract* from your compass course the number of *degrees east*. If you are *west*, the *degrees west are added*.

This may seem awesomely complicated. Fortunately, it isn't, because some maps, which we will discuss shortly, note the declination for the area they cover. More valuable to the traveler who takes trips in many locations is a declination chart available from the U.S. Printing Office in Washington, that gives by map the declinations, for any point in the U.S. It is essential to have this chart any time you are using a map without the declination noted on it.

Suppose you have such a map, without noted declinations. Place your compass on it, and line it up so the compass needle is parallel with one of the meridian lines that runs *map* north-south; then move the map so the needle is pointing at the number of degrees given in the declination chart for this area. The needle is now pointing True North. With the orienting compass I have described, you do not move the map but instead turn the compass housing to the proper number of degrees shown on the declination chart for this location.

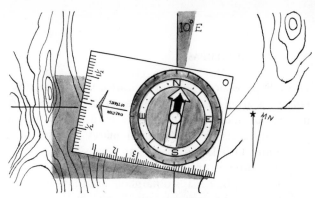

It is important to adjust your compass to allow for the magnetic declination between Magnetic North and True North. With your compass placed on the map, line up N and S on the compass with the north-south line on the map indicating True North. Next, rotate the map and compass until the needle lines up with the map's Magnetic North line. If your map does not have a Magnetic North line, use a declination chart to determine the number of degrees necessary to correct for your area, and turn the map and compass so the needle is the proper number of degrees east or west of True North.

Reading Maps

Now to maps. For short jaunts in settled territory, ordinary road maps, if they are up-to-date, are handy enough. But they won't do for wilderness trips, or even for a day's hunt in a State Forest. Many states have excellent county maps, and most have State Forest maps. National Forest maps also are excellent. Some large Forests have detail maps showing only specified sectors. National Forest maps are obtainable from the

Forest Supervisor of a particular area, from a Regional Office, or from the Washington, D.C. Forest Service main office. State maps of counties are usually available at county seats or state capital offices. Forestry and Game and Fish Departments can furnish State Forest maps and often county maps.

Among the best maps obtainable are those from the U.S. Geological Survey, and the Canadian Department of Mines. These are the topographic maps that show specific areas in great detail. They have carefully plotted elevation contours, most useful. Once you learn to read these, you can get a good mental picture of the surrounding country, know where obstacles such as cliffs or steep mountains are, and so on. These maps utilize a standard marking code system, and you should study it so that you know what the symbols mean: a marsh, a spring, what tints are used on woodland issues to indicate types of forest and brush, what various roads and trails are like for quality.

Each of these maps has a diagram on the bottom that shows the magnetic declination for the specific map region, both in degrees and with lines indicating True and Magnetic North. These lines, projected upward across the map face, drawn in if you wish, are most useful. The maps are also *dated;* the date means that the map was made the year of the date. Be sure to get maps as up-to-date as possible. Otherwise changes since that date—new roads or trails, buildings or ranger stations, etc.—may not show on the map and will be confusing to you. If you have to use an older Geological or Geodetic Survey map, it still will get you there and back.

Just don't be too concerned if you find something that's not on the map.

These maps are made up in differing scales: an inch to a mile, an inch to 2,000 feet, an inch to several miles. In most usage the smaller the area covered by the map and the smaller the scale, that is, the smaller the distance covered by an inch, the more information it will give you. If you feel you need Geological Survey maps, you can get a list of them for the state or province in question from the Washington or Ottawa sources mentioned. Then you pick the ones you want and order them, at stipulated fees. In average instances in the U.S., outdoorsmen will be going into State or National Forests, and the standard maps from the State or the Forest Service will do very nicely. But for all the fine points, and the contours, the others are better.

Map and Compass Together

When using any map out in the field, always take your compass reading and then lay the map out so it is turned in the *proper direction*. Then you see precisely what is where. If you aren't sure exactly what your position is, but can locate both visually and on your map two identifiable points, such as mountains, you can easily "find" yourself. Get a degree reading on one landmark, then on the other. Place your compass on the map, and orient map and compass for the first reading. Draw a line from the landmark back in the direction from which you are sighting. Repeat, using the second reading. You are at the point where the two

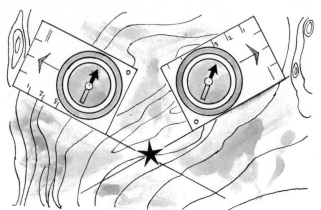

When you are uncertain of your position in the field, but you can locate visually and on your map two landmarks, you will have no trouble finding yourself. Take a degree reading for the first point, and with your compass on the map, adjust map and compass to this reading. Draw a line on the map from the landmark you just identified back in the direction from which you took the reading. Repeat the procedure for the second point. You are standing at the point where the two lines intersect on the map.

lines will cross. Now that you know precisely your position, you can forge ahead to some predetermined destination, or you can get a bearing back toward vehicle or camp. Two rules you must always follow are to *believe your compass,* and at all times *to know where you are on your map.* To be sure, compass readings in some situations are upset by metal, in the ground or in your equipment. But the chance is not great. Get away from your metals while taking readings.

In using the orienting-type compass, don't fail to work with the measuring edges on the flat base. Often you can place the base on your map so that the long measuring edge touches your *location* and *destination*. The *sighting arrow* on the base will then be pointing in your direction. If you have prepared your map ahead of time by drawing in parallel lines at intervals showing Magnetic North, all you have to do is turn the housing until the drawn-in pointing arrow on the bottom of the housing is parallel to the Magnetic North lines, and you have the degree reading for your course.

There is much more that can be learned about use of map and compass. But these are the fundamentals. Study your map thoroughly beforehand and during any trip. Use your compass often. *Memorize landmarks* and keep *looking back.*

6 / Travel in the Wilderness

It is not just when you are lost that you need a set of general rules on what to do and what not to do when traveling in the outdoors. The rules that follow will help you both to avoid certain emergencies and to extricate yourself efficiently when you do have one.

I once met a lost man in a State Forest in Michigan. When he found me he was wet from crossing a river. He had simply stumbled upon me. Had he heard me or seen me and crossed a river to reach me, his action would have been legitimate. But the fact that he crossed the stream some time earlier illustrates an error to avoid. If you are one side of a stream and have left your car, as he had, "somewhere back there," all you can possibly accomplish by crossing the stream is to get yourself more lost than ever.

The stream in this instance was a very definite boundary. Even though the man didn't have any idea where he was, he should have considered the fact that he was *somewhere between the road and the river.* This at least gave him something to tie to. Once he crossed it, though, he was "out of the pasture."

Following Water

With map and compass and a useful *knowledge of both,* this person could not have become lost in the first place. But at times either one or all are missing. If you become lost without these, one of the *do nots* is *do not cross a stream.* A better idea is to follow it. Streams run downhill and for centuries they have been guidelines for wilderness travelers. Many have trails near them or right beside them. Streams may be crossed by trails and bridges and roads and railroads and high-lines. A stream is something to cling to.

In most instances you should not try to walk close to it. Vegetation grows densely along most streams. Swamps and bogs spread out from a stream at some locations. The stream may twist and loop and turn, making your hike much longer. Unless there is a streamside trail, it is best to parallel a stream a short distance away, and from a ridge top if there is one, where you can see it or its valley course most of the time.

Any outdoorsman worth his salt should know in which general direction a stream is flowing. Somehow misinformation got started long ago that only a very few streams flow north. This is nonsense. In the Arctic

most of them flow north, and straight away from settlement. In the northern part of Michigan's Lower Peninsula, the group of streams flows in a northerly direction. If a hunter is aware of that by map study, and
knows even a little bit about the country he is in, he
knows whether to go upstream or downstream.

In the West, where the largest expanses of wilderness are located, chiefly in National Forests, stream direction is an excellent clue to general orientation. From
atop the Continental Divide all the length of the
Rockies, streams flow downhill on the west side toward
the Pacific and downhill on the east slope toward the
Mississippi and the Gulf of Mexico. Any time you
travel downstream you know that eventually you come
to larger streams to which the one you are following is
tributary. And eventually, too, you will enter valleys
that have settlement, either farms or ranches or villages.
The hike certainly could be a long one. But on either
side of the Divide, a totally lost man should always go
downhill, downstream.

In some cases it is an oversimplification to say you
should go "west downhill" or "east downhill." There
are many individual drainages where this wouldn't
work. I think offhand of a block of the Santa Fe National Forest east of Santa Fe, New Mexico, in which
the Pecos Wilderness Area is located. The Pecos River
cuts south through these handsome mountains. Its
canyon is a main topographic landmark. Tributaries
come into it from *both sides*. Thus, if you were on the
east side of the Wilderness you would follow a creek
downstream southwest to hit the main river, and vice
versa. In other words, do know the *watershed* of the

region so you have its general pattern well fixed in your mind.

Don't make hasty decisions, lost or not. Be sure you are right. When lost, or in a situation where you have to walk out, don't rush. Conserve energy. Take it slow. If you were on a ten-day trip, make believe you still wish to spend that time. Don't compound your trouble by hurting yourself. Hunters, particularly those who get lost easily, will even find that using map and compass is a good idea. You don't need to hunt *aimlessly,* wandering. In forests from Maine to Ontario to Montana to Arizona, an old and unused log trail, a stream course, a lake shore offers just as good hunting as you find plunging off into unmarked territory that all looks alike. It may even be better because of the opening of the trail, and edge habitat. The log trail or stream or lakeshore gives you something to *tie to,* and to follow back to camp or use as a known point of orientation.

By the same token, if you are lost or having to walk out of an emergency, unless you are very sure of yourself and your ability with map and compass, don't strike out cross-country. In the woods, *there are no shortcuts!* If there is a trail, stay on it. Avoid cross-country travel unless it is absolutely necessary. An exception might be striking across an area on a ridge from which you know or can see that a stream meanders endlessly.

Starting Out

When you set up your camp, or park your vehicle—whatever your *starting* point—don't place it at some indiscriminate spot. Have it *somewhere*. Most campers will set up at a recognized campsite—there are many in the National and State Forests—or they will camp near a stream or lake. The smart vehicle operator will park near a bridge, let's say, and hunt one side of the river. Or he will leave the car near an intersection, or a high-line or railroad crossing. In other words, such starting points give you a definite *place to come back to*.

I recall a campsite several of us had one year in the San Juan Primitive Area in Colorado. It was a lovely spot at the confluence of a tributary stream with the main river. By hunting in the morning climbing uphill, we gave ourselves the advantage of a downhill run when we were tired out later in the day. We were also hunting in a tract that was bounded on two sides by streams. We knew the main river was flowing almost straight south, the tributary east by south. If we climbed the slope on the south side of the tributary, wherever we quit we could set a course and hit one of the streams. Northeast or north would have us converging on the tributary, or straight east we'd hit one or the other. If we hit the main river, we knew we had to go upstream to find camp because it was at the confluence and we had not crossed the tributary. If we hit the tributary, we knew we had to go downstream until we got to the main river.

You won't always have it quite that neat. On a road or stream where you aren't "boxed in," finding camp can be harder than that even when you know where you are. You follow a certain compass course, let's say, hiking to a high lake to fish. But even if you follow the same one going back, probably you won't hit right on the nose. So, when you do find stream or road or trail where camp is, which way should you go on it? This is a problem you can lick by purposely taking yourself off course a bit. If, for example, you know camp should be straight south, set a course a few degrees to the east or west. This assures that you'll strike road or stream where camp or car is located a short distance from it in a *known direction*. Of course, if you have looked back often and have your landmarks well in mind, this isn't necessary.

Not only should your real camp or parking place be easy to locate, but when you make any other camp during an emergency, choose a location which is easy to find your way back to if necessary.

When To Stay Put

We talked previously of panic. Don't. If you are lost, stop where you are the moment you realize it. Don't move again until you are calm and have done your best to puzzle out your location, and the error you made to get there. Study your map again, use your compass. If you aren't sure and it is late in the day, stay there. In the morning things will look better. Mark *this spot* well, range out after a landmark to tie to, like a stream, and make, if necessary, a permanent, come-back-to camp there.

"Staying put" is often what you should do to help yourself. If you have some difficulty in the desert, and you are by a waterhole, don't move. If you have left word, as you should have, you will be found. If you are not at a waterhole, and have a broken-down vehicle, get in the shade beside it or under it and make your-self comfortable, conserving your energy and what water you have. Stay right there until someone finds you.

There are instances when storms wipe out trails and you don't know where to point your vehicle. Park it and stay put. This is an absolute for the plane crash victim. Even if you are injured only slightly, you compound the difficulty if you try to walk out. The crashed plane is easier to spot than you will be. The same applies to boats and canoes. If you are cracked up many miles from settlement, and someone knows where you were going and when you were to be back, it is best to stay with the craft and let searchers find it, and you. There are exceptions, when you are close to settlement and know it and were to be gone a long time. You must use careful judgment The rule: if you have any doubt whatever, stay put.

Following Trails

Some writers concerned with survival have suggested following game trails where possible for easy going. In my opinion this is precisely what *not* to do. There are a few exceptions. A bear trail may be an easy way through a small dense thicket. A caribou trail may take you where you are going, if you know their migration routes in that area. But game isn't usually going where you are, nor for the same purposes. Get on a deer trail sometime and follow it. Many of them are as aimless as trails left by lost men. For helter-skelter try a bear trail over some distance. My advice about game trails is to utilize one when it suits *your* purpose, but never to follow one because you think it is "going somewhere."

I have mentioned sticking to the ridges in mountain or hill country. Never walk up when you can walk level. Conserve energy. At times, climbing to a ridge top is better than walking along the side of a slope because you don't fight one "short leg," and there will be less interference from down timber. Much of the down timber, in forests where it is plentiful, will be lying on a general downhill slant. Walking along a slope thus forces you constantly to climb over. It is exhausting.

Unless it is absolutely necessary, never attempt to cross unfamiliar swamps or bogs. They can compound trouble, are at best exhausting. If you have a crackup of some kind—with an airboat for example in a spot like the Everglades—stay where you are until found. Many persons get into trouble in the high country of the West with horses, because they don't realize that there are some fantastic bogholes even way up at and above timberline. These may look innocuous, but you can sink a horse to its belly in an instant if you force the mount across. Skirt all low, moist spots, even way up at the top.

Snakes

Outdoorsmen must be continually alert against snake trouble. Rattlesnakes are the most common of the poisonous species, and most widespread. Cottonmouths are predominantly southern in range, usually found near water, and in some cases in the Southeast U.S. in large numbers. They are likely to be more aggressive

Rattlesnake

Water Moccasin

Copperhead

Coral Snake

Learn to identify the poisonous snakes in the
area you will be in, and watch out for them.
The most common species are shown at left.

than rattlesnakes. Copperheads, though smaller, range
widely and can be dangerous, especially when you are
unable to receive prompt treatment. Coral snakes are
deadly, but are burrowers and not fanged like the
others; they're chewers. It is seldom that anyone is
bitten by a coral snake except by handling it.

States where the most snakebites annually occur are:
Florida, Georgia, Alabama, Louisiana, Mississippi, Mis-
souri, Arkansas, Texas, Oklahoma, Virginia, North
Carolina, West Virginia, and California. South Carolina, Arizona, Kansas, Tennessee and Kentucky are
next. The mountain states, where so many sportsmen
visit National Forests and other public lands, all regis-
ter a substantial number of snakebites annually. There
are also a few in the Dakotas, and in the Great Lakes
states. Canada has a few cases. Although surveys show
that sportsmen are by no means the most frequently
bitten group, because of the potential danger you
should always be alert to and know the basic rules for
avoiding snakes.

Never reach into holes such as animal burrows. Never
reach up when climbing to grasp a ledge, above and
past which you are unable to see. Don't put your face
near a ledge from which a snake could strike. Be extremely cautious in snake country about stepping over
a log or a rock. Step up on them. Beware of jumping
off a jutting rock under which a snake may lie. In my
home region in Texas I am extremely wary of such

places as armadillo burrows, which are often under the edge of an uptilted slab of rock. Not long ago I was walking with a friend who stepped atop just such a slab. I had seen burrow entrance dirt as I started

Don't be careless in snake country: (1) never reach into holes; (2) don't jump over a log that may hide a snake underneath; (3) avoid sitting against ledges from which a snake could strike.

around. I started to yell, "Don't step off!" But before I could do so a snake buzzed its rattles wildly. He stepped back safely. Unfortunately, not all of them give a warning.

Don't move around the corner of a shady, creviced ledge without looking at where your feet and legs will be. Always look closely before you sit down on a log, a rock, or on the gound. A high percentage of snake-bites occur from carelessness. When it is hot, in an area where snakes are common, walk in the bright places. Snakes coil in shade. Be chary of walking in tall weeds. Watch closely around abandoned buildings, caves, packrat nests. Be especially wary as dusk comes on and heat subsides. This is when snakes begin to move. Walking after dark in desert and other areas where rattlers are common is not a good idea. When gathering dead wood for fires, look before you reach. Watch those debris piles and hollow logs.

In boats or when fishing in swamps where cotton-mouths are common, it isn't just the ground that's dangerous. They love to lie on limbs. Don't push a boat in swiftly under branches without checking every-thing carefully. If you hang a lure in weeds, probe with a paddle first before reaching. One time in Florida I started to reach for a bass bug I'd hung on a water hyacinth and there lay an enormous cottonmouth. In Georgia on the Flint River I reached out to seize a limb as a partner maneuvered a boat to shore, and there was a big one on the very limb.

One of the most important "don'ts" is this: don't forget that snakes can be where you least expect them. For example, making a hands-and-knees or belly-crawl-ing stalk on an antelope in New Mexico or Wyoming can be dangerous. In some parts of Nebraska bird hunt-ers who've never seen a rattler before find some they wish they hadn't, almost every fall. The most important "do" concerning snakes: Carry a snakebit kit at all times, even on a day's outing, and study the treatment instructions included with it thoroughly beforehand. In addition, *you can carry antivenin,* and administer it to yourself if need be. A druggist can order an antivenin kit for you if he does not carry them. In "back-in" situations such a kit can be a lifesaver.

Horse Know-how

Outdoorsmen get themselves into difficulty with horses and mules, on pack-in trips. Nowadays so few people have contact with horses that most know little about handling them. Stay away from the "business" end, the rear. Don't even walk around the rear of horse or mule. Skirt it widely. Never come up suddenly from any angle. Be sure the animal knows you are there. Even the most docile old trail plug can come apart when startled. Never approach from the right side. Horses are trained to expect you to saddle them, put a bridle on, and mount, *from the left.* We have raised a number of horses, broken a few and ridden a good many. What you eventually find out is that you really never know *all* about what the gentlest nag may do. Just remember, neither do they!

Watch closely when you are starting on a pack-in to see how your outfitter handles the stock. Familiarize

Handle horses carefully. Tether to a movable log whenever you must leave; stake to the ground at night to allow grazing in a limited range. Know how to hobble the horse with buckled straps or light twisted rawhide for extra protection against wandering. Never approach ny horse from the rear.

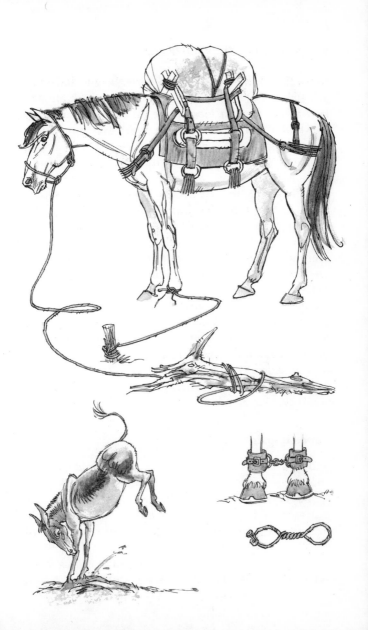

yourself with how to hobble a horse, how to stake out a "catch horse," how to lash a pack on a pack animal, how to approach a loose horse, in case in emergency you find a stray. Probably you won't ever have to do these things, but it is good knowledge to have.

When you ride and are not used to riding, get down every half hour and walk a bit. I've seen some riders literally unable to walk because they stayed in a saddle too long at a time. It's your *knees* that will give you trouble. Your rear end will just get sore but it won't cripple you. Suffer gracefully. But a bit of walking every half hour will keep you limbered up. When you are sore and stiff after the first day, go right at it again. Believe me, this is the best cure. And sit flat in your saddle. By easing your backside while sitting up on the rear flange of your saddle, or by slouching to one side for hours at a time, you can cripple your horse. You can do the same by hanging a heavy pack off the horn on one side. Keep a balanced load. The old cayuse under you is the best friend in the wilderness that you'll ever have!

Canoe Repair

If you are to travel by canoe, you should have in your gear a repair kit for the material of which the canoe is made. They are available for fiberglass and for canvas-covered canoes. Aluminum presents some problem, but is more likely to be bent than rent. A small puncture can be filled with pine resin, or plugged by pulling a hunk of cloth through and snipping both sides fairly close. However, if you can locate any in stores, get a few tubes of what is called "liquid aluminum solder." This is soft, and is smoothed across a puncture on both sides and the hole filled with it. I once repaired a small craft I used for floating fast rivers that way, and when I sold that little floater a half-dozen years later the plug was still in place.

Vehicular Travel

Nowadays vehicular travel in wilderness situations is popular. The 4WD vehicles can go a great many places. All vehicles, however, from short-4 to trail bike to snowmobile to the newer ATVs, are troublemakers at one time or another. I always feel far more secure on horseback. If I had a dollar an hour for all the time I've spent over the years getting "unstuck" or "un-broke-down" I could spend a few months doing nothing!

The subject of vehicular travel "back in" is vast, and there is room here only to touch a scattering of essentials. When you buy a vehicle, choose carefully. Most ATVs are more expensive playthings than rough-country transport. A pickup truck can go a lot of places, but its lack of rear-end weight handicaps it. This excepts the 4WD pickup. Trail bikes are not very comfortable or practical. Unquestionably the best rough use vehicles are the short-wheelbase four-wheel-drives.

Breakdowns. Most mechanical breakdown problems are with the electrical systems, fuel pumps, and belts. Carry spare parts for all—pump, belts, distributor, coil, plugs, points, etc.—and study the systems and their repair beforehand. You should have a well-selected assortment of tools, in a good waterproof box. Tires also give trouble. See that you get the best for the terrain where you'll use them most. Carry two spares, and repair tools and equipment.

The other two most common problems are getting stuck, and puncturing an oil pan on rocks. These can cause such awesome difficulties at times that I cannot imagine anyone's failing to shell out the cash to cure them. That's all it takes. If you can afford the vehicle, you can afford the cure.

Tools. A good winch, even though it costs two- or three-hundred dollars, is worth more than the whole vehicle when you are really bogged. There are several types of cheaper "come-alongs" that work fairly well. But a powerful winch saves hours of back-breaking labor and gets you out of snow, mud or sand when you absolutely could not get out any other way. It can also save a vehicle that has slipped off onto a steep slope from catapulting over a cliff as you try to ease back up. You can hook up to trees, boulders, even bushes.

Recently a group of us hunting near the Mexican border after a hard rain were unmercifully hung up with a 4WD pickup. When you get a 4WD stuck, you know you *are* stuck. Novices think a 4WD can go anywhere. It can't. It just sticks harder! We hauled a long length of cable off the winch, hooked to the only item in reach, a skinny clump of scrub mesquite. If you place a cable around bushes *right at ground level,* and ease on the power very gently, it is amazing what hold the roots have. We were out in no time. Be sure a winch is outfitted with plenty of cable.

To avoid oil pan trouble, and gas tank and gas line

too, all it takes is welding steel plates beneath. I have been up on rocks where the front wheels were turning in air, the front end weight sitting on a steel plate right below the oil pan. This addition is so simple and so valuable that no 4WD traveler should be without it. Most of the time, however, if outdoorsmen using vehicles would just exercise caution, and think carefully before crossing spots that look bad, they wouldn't need either winch or steel plates.

Husky jacks should be carried. You should also have an engine air pump and spark-plug wrench, and a tire gauge that reads low pressures. In sand, letting down to ten or twelve pounds tire pressure will usually get you out if you move the vehicle gingerly. Chains for all four wheels of the 4WD, a shovel, and an axe are all mandatory extras. Bailing wire, too. You can easily bridge a bad mudhole by cutting four logs, binding two pairs together and laying them across for wheel tracks. The wheels of the vehicle will creep across in the V formed where each pair of rounded logs comes together. But go slowly!

As noted earlier, don't be hasty about leaving your vehicle if it is hopelessly broken down. If you've done as you should—notified someone of your trip plans beforehand, and followed through on it—by staying with your vehicle you will be found. Also, at the vehicle you have everything you need. You can utilize various signals to assist those who will be searching for you, or to attract those who may be near and unaware of your difficulty. There is a chapter about signaling later in this book.

Short Forages

Remember to make camps at places to which you can easily find your way back. However, a breakdown of a vehicle, a plane crash, loss of a horse, even becoming lost may suddenly place you where you have no choice about your immediate campsite. In order not to become more lost, and to avoid ranging out from a vehicle or plane till you are unable to find it again, there is a definite procedure to follow.

Suppose that you are near a stream, or on a lakeshore, or in a broad valley at the foot of a ridge, or up on the ridge itself. Any known lines—stream, shoreline, valley, ridge—give you an exact two-directional foraging area. That is, if you go up the shore and stick to it, you can come back to camp without fail. Then you can explore from camp down the shore in the opposite direction. In a broad valley, stay at the foot of the ridge and you can come back to camp (vehicle, place where you first knew you were lost) without any trouble. The same goes for ridge top or stream course.

You may need to make excursions of a half-mile to two miles, seeking food, or water, or material for shelter. When you make such excursions, stick to the *known line;* don't wander. Note landmarks, bends in a stream, pockets of vegetation, anything and everything that you will be able to identify later. Look *back* at each after passing. This is what you'll see on return. Traveling one of these *known lines* out and back—in a desert it could be a dry wash or foot of a mountain or rock wall—is the *only* jaunt you should take until you are completely familiar with the area.

When you are familiar, you can set a compass course at right angles for forage trips. That is, if you are at the foot of a ridge in a wide valley, set your course out across the valley, and return to the ridge. Walking may be such that you won't hit exactly where you had hoped

Set a compass course for short forage trips **only** when you are familiar with the natural features and landmarks of the immediate area.

to when you come back to the ridge. But because you checked out that ridge base in both directions from camp, you will know by landmarks where you are and which way to go. You are now totally oriented, at least in this vicinity. And you know something of the country around you. If lost, you might find yourself while making these side trips. If waiting for rescue, you are able to find food and other necessities. There is hardly anyplace that does not have some kind of known line to cling to.

Choosing Ridge or Stream

I have mentioned staying on the ridges or along streams, rather than trying to travel "against the grain" by climbing up and over one ridge after another and

> In ridge and stream country, a travel line along the ridge which keeps the stream in sight provides the most helpful overall view.

crossing the valleys and streams. The given terrain will of course influence whether you choose a ridge or a stream. The stream gives you water and infinitely more opportunities to find food than the ridge top. But it may be rougher traveling unless there is a trail. Consider that climbing a ridge above a stream gives you a look at the surrounding country and better orientation. Often from a ridge top you can get a fair look at what is ahead of you downstream. Be careful when traveling a ridge, however, not to become confused by other spurs and broken ridges that come in.

If you have a binocular, glass long and carefully. You may spot a swamp filling a looping bend of the stream, or a vertical rock wall on your side, or an area of streamside brush jungle which, were you to enter it, might be difficult to get through and easy to get lost in. You may see in the distance a tributary coming into the main stream that you otherwise would have to cross. In any of these instances, the travel line should be along the ridge, but with the stream in sight. Thus you circumvent the need to cross a swamp or a patch of jungle, to climb again to get around a rock wall, or to get across a large tributary.

Flat country. You may be in flat country. Streams there are frequently slower than mountain streams, and seldom have falls or difficult rapids. Vegetation is usually dense near the stream. If you can keep the stream in view, or even the dense vegetation line that follows it, and travel at some distance away, you will avoid having to plow through tangles of vines, brush, weeds and forest. However, a stream of even modest size can *be* a travel route, if you can fashion some sort of raft.

Mountain streams. On exceeding swift, rocky mountain streams with extreme gradient, rafting attempts are simply foolhardy. If you are going into strange country, know beforehand something of stream character. Many states furnish booklets about their wilderness streams, with specifics about which stretches are good canoe water and where impassable or dangerous rapids or falls occur. If you know where you are, but are in an emergency situation where you have to get out under your own power, knowledge of the streams is invaluable. If you do not have such knowledge, forget rafting attempts on any stream of a general character that appears to you too rough or dangerous. The whole idea is to stay alive and uninjured. Your chances are better on foot.

Building a Raft

Fortunately, on most streams where traveling via raft is feasible, materials for building one will be most common. It is along the lower-altitude meandering streams of modest current that the most vines and pliable brush stalks grow. If you intend to try rafting, don't rush your building job, and consider carefully what you use. Water-soaked logs won't float. Several varieties of wood also do not float even when dry, or else float poorly. In lumber days in Michigan, where much black walnut grew, immensely valuable booms were often lost because the heavy, high-density walnut logs would not float. If the flotation logs around them broke free, down they went.

Logs. For the quickest and easiest raft-building job you need dry logs, preferably of soft wood. Be sure they are not rotted or they will soak swiftly. Green logs of standing conifers can be cut, but they are heavy and difficult to handle. If you have no cutting tool, you can

Build a rectangular raft by lashing crossbars to logs, using diagonal brace lashed to crossbars to add rigidity. Increase raft strength by lashing together the overhanging ends of two crossbars at each end of the raft.

burn standing trees by the Indian method of a fire ring at the base. But be warned, it is a slow, tedious process and not worth the effort if makeshift materials are available. You must plaster a thick ring of wet mud around the trunk several feet up from the ground. Then you build a fire around the base. The mud is kept wet, and as the trunk burns the charred portions are hacked off with sharp stones, if that is all you have, or with a hatchet. Once the tree is down, sections are burned off by building small hot fires under the trunk at intervals. I think of this entire task as a last-resort for moving an injured person. A healthy man can walk farther for the amount of energy expended than he probably would float.

Lashings. Don't look for huge raft logs. Use those about six inches in diameter. They're easy to handle, easier to lash together, and do not so readily break makeshift lashings. If one does break away, assuming the raft has been built to hold *more* than required weight, which it should be, the rider is still safe. Presumably you will have lashing material in your pack— rope, rawhide thongs. If not, careful work with vines, or even with selected bundles of cattails or strong grasses, or bark strips, will hold a raft together. These can also supplement what lashings you do have. Strips of green inner bark, from cedar, basswood, some of the oaks, make excellent cordage. (See Chapter 10 on making fish lines for other cordage ideas.) If these are soaked for some time in water, the fibers can be separated easily. However, most emergencies do not allow that much time. Nettles and reeds, when braided into strands, are very strong. Yucca leaves are tough as rope, although in most rafting situations—but not all—these plants would not be present.

Never try to build a square raft. Make it a long rectangle. It will handle better. Also, build it at water's edge. If it will be heavy, build it upon two slanted supporting logs down which it can be skidded for launching. Any jerry-built raft should have base logs, with crisscross smaller material atop if possible, to give the rafter a high-and-dry seat. Be sure the outer edges

A light but sturdy pushpole keeps you going through slow current, prevents obstacles from stopping travel.

of the raft have the most buoyant, largest logs. This helps stability. By all means launch in a slack pool if it is possible. Then test the raft before pushing off into current.

A pushpole is mandatory. Cut a green one, light but sturdy, of a length related to general depth of the stream. Use it for primitive guidance, for assistance in slow current, and for fending off from obstructions or bank. If you are on a broad, deep river, try for a pole ten feet long. Also take with you some sort of make-shift paddle, a square of green, heavy bark, a light, dry flat stick. This assists you if a slow, deep hole or back-eddy becalms your raft.

In warm water, you can make a small temporary raft for brief crossings or for getting around a swamp or other difficult going by lashing a tarp or backpack tent, or even clothing, over a frame of logs. There is a caution here, however. Weigh your decision to try this very carefully, as you might better go the long way around than chance losing your gear by poor lashing or a makeshift float not quite buoyant enough.

Wading Streams

Crossing streams by wading may be necessary in numerous situations. Even on slow streams, use a staff, a *green* stick sizable enough so it will not bend with your leaning weight. You cannot wade a swift stream safely if the water is above your hips, and many streams with extreme gradients cannot be waded if water is much above your knees. If you are unused to swift water, note this well! In crossing, keep sideways to the current or nearly so, turned just enough downstream to point on a diagonal. This places the least leg or body resistance against the water and allows you to move gently with the push of the current, pushed downstream while taking diagonal steps across. Brace the staff on the downstream side.

Use a wading stick to cross a stream. In swift water, travel sideways to the current, facing your body on a diagonal downstream.

In rocky streams, be wary of holes as well as slippery rocks. If current is slow enough so you can stand quietly, probe with your staff to find good footing. Also be wary of soft deep-muck spots in slow streams. Most of these will be back-eddied into the inside of a bend. However, do not try to cross any stream of fair depth on a diagonal headed for the *outside* of a bend. This is where the deeper water will invariably be. The outside bend may also have eroded away so a vertical bank is present. This can be a trap. Try to cross on straightaway stretches, as a rule. And on a fast stream the wider stretches will usually be the shallowest.

Swimming. Emergencies may require swimming or floating across a stream. In such instances, equipment will get wet. And it may be all but impossible to cross with equipment. Nonetheless, you should know the basic rules for swimming various types of streams. In modest current and in case you are not a very good swimmer, shoving out a log and crossing with it as support is possible. Stay on the upstream side of the log. In swimming any stream, be exceedingly wary of cold water. It will numb you faster than you believe.

In a swift run that you are sure is deep, swim face down, headed downstream. In a shallow, swift run lie on your back and go feet first. Never fight a current; simply go with it and keep angling across. Get buoyancy assistance from your clothing. Trousers tied at the ankles, thoroughly wet in the stream then wrung gently, swung around your head to scoop in air, and then snugged at top to trap the air can form a make-shift "waterwing."

All of these ideas, however, have their hazards. It is worthwhile to know them, but remember that attempts to cross a stream that is not readily wadeable, or raft-able, may only add to your problems. If at all possible, avoid such crossings. Be absolutely certain the crossing is necessary, and that no other land-based plan is possible. By no means should you take a chance on losing your most valuable possessions—gear you are carrying—in a stream crossing. If that is even a mild possibility, look for another way!

Natural Hazards

Ice, quicksand, various bogs are all dangers to avoid by every means, even if a much longer trek results. However, if it is absolutely necessary to cross such places, here are a few suggestions. Ice may be thick and strong, but don't take chances. On streams there may

The best way to cross ice is to lie flat and crawl. A long pole stretched at right angles in front of you will give support in case the ice cracks.

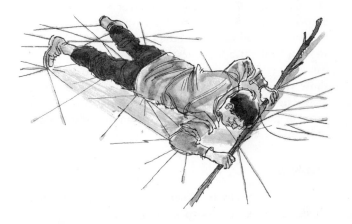

be soft pockets or open places; on lakes, springholes on bottom in shallow water may make soft spots. If you think the ice may not be well formed and of uniform thickness, don't walk. Instead crawl with a "swimming" motion, arms and legs wide to distribute weight. Better still, lie flat and carry a long pole, held in the middle and at right angles to your body. It will support you if ice cracks. In any variety of quagmire—quicksand or muck—don't try to stand up, which only keeps you sinking deeper. Get flat out on your stomach, and *swim* or crawl, through it.

The best idea is not to get into such places. Quicksand, if found along stream courses, is only localized. It will not support even small gravel-sized stones, so beware of watery-appearing sand with no stones on top. Thrust a stick into it to test it. Do likewise with muck. Most bogs or quagmires anywhere on the continent where emergencies are likely to occur are easily skirted. If you get into one in error, and it has tussocks of heavy marsh grass, plus some brush such as alders, step onto the tussocks and in the middle of the alder bushes, one step carefully at a time, test for support. Look around carefully at distant vegetation, particularly trees. These show you the closest way to high ground. Tamarack grows in bog situations. So does willow. But pine or birch or poplar, for example, grow on firm ground and indicate the edge of the bog.

Climbing

Attempts to climb either up or down cliffs, and climbing trees for lookout sites, are two very pre-

If a rescue team lets down a rope to you along the side of a cliff, one way to secure it around your body is to make a loop at the end of the rope, large enough to stand in. Bring the loop up to your chest, and pass the rest of the rope through the chest loop.

carious undertakings when you are in an emergency situation. Avoid both if at all possible, because they may lead to injuries or compound your difficulties. Nonetheless, basic rules are a part of survival repertoire. For example, if you have been in a plane crash, you can make rope from parachute shroud lines by twisting several together. Perhaps you carried a long rope when going into mountain country. It can get you down a cliff, if that is absolutely necessary.

Select a tree or rock outcrop at the edge of the descent point. A tree must be sturdy, and a rock must be

without any question solid enough to sustain your weight. Pass the rope around this snubbing point exactly at mid-length, so the two ends, one on either side, are even. They *must* reach to destination point down below with a few feet left over. Be positive about this. Otherwise you'll wind up down over a cliff and dangling well above the valley floor!

Pass the rope, both strands, through your crotch from the front. That is, straddle it. Then bring it around across one hip, up across your chest and over the opposite shoulder. Suppose you have brought it around the left hip and up over the right shoulder. Your right hand now grasps both strands, between the snubbing point and the crotch. Where the ropes pass across the right shoulder, bring them around behind your back and let the left hand grasp them at the lower left side. Now as you descend, keeping feet against whatever holds are possible, rope is slowly paid out through the left hand, and the right hand. The friction allows a slow, secure descent. This is known in

When you must get down a cliff, use a long rope anchored safely to the descent point. For rappelling down steep areas, a double rope goes under one thigh and across the opposite shoulder. Grasp both strands with right hand if the rope is over your right shoulder. Bring the ropes behind your back, holding them at the lower left side with the left hand. Now with feet against whatever holds are possible, descend by letting rope out slowly through the left and then right hand. Make sure the rope reaches the destination point with some left over.

climbing terminology as "rappelling." You should be certain when looping the rope around the snubbing point that it will not bind. Thus, when you reach the lower elevation at cliff base, a pull on one strand retrieves the rope.

No climbing up or down should be attempted without using every precaution. Face a cliff or steep spot. Test every hold thoroughly. Watch out for any loose rock if you are going downward. Shove loose rocks off ledges, so they will not fall on you later. When traveling not necessarily on ledges and cliffs but over steep shale slides, keep your feet spaced well apart and avoid by any means starting to slide. It is better to avoid such places, even if going around means a longer hike. As we have said often, dodging possible danger is better than facing it!

Trees. You may find it necessary to climb a tree, such as a smooth-trunked palm. Natives do this by tying a short rope between the ankles. The hands and arms encircle the trunk, and the feet, kept apart and ankles pressed against the rope, are hunched up and braced as one climbs. You might be able to use this technique to get up a tall pine or aspen with no lower limbs. But this is a test of strength, uses an immense amount of energy, and the advantages may not equal the necessary effort. A tree with a limbless trunk too large for you to reach around is a poor bet for climbing anyway. If you must climb to get your bearings, try to select an "easy" tree, where limbs grow near the ground. Never put your weight out *on* a limb. Keep it right next to the trunk. Even a dead limb you misjudge as alive is more likely to bear your weight at the point where it joins the trunk. Select a tree with numerous limbs, for the least amount of exertion. Except in a dense, flat country where you wish to obtain some bearing or spot a landmark, there is seldom valid reason for climbing tall trees.

When traveling in the wilderness, what *to* do is certainly important, but it seems to me that the "don'ts" are even more important. Two of the highest importance, I think, are these: Whatever happens, don't panic; and, never go into wilderness situations alone. Invariably it is the loner who gets into the worst predicaments, simply because there is no one to assist!

7 / Where to Find Water

In any climate where severe cold does not drain energy, you can live for many days without a single bite of food. The length of time depends to some extent upon how much physical energy must be expended. Starving to death is not as dangerous as finding yourself without water. Charts have been compiled showing average life expectancy without water.

Temperature is crucial here. Even in the desert, where you may encounter extreme high temperatures to well above 100 degrees, a man who remains quiet and in shade can go without water a short time. Expectancy would be from two to three days. At moderate summer temperatures in woodland latitudes, say from 50 to 75 degrees, death might not occur for ten days, but before that a man would become too sick to help himself.

Water is the most important factor in survival, regardless of where you are. It is estimated that at 110-degree temperature, an inactive person lives for 5 days if he has available 2 quarts of water per day, a total of 10 quarts. At about 75 degrees he has a chance of quadrupling his life expectancy on the same 10 quarts. But these are bare minimums and this is also a substantial quantity of water. At a moderate temperature a person even mildly active needs an average of 2 quarts of water per day. That's 3½ gallons per week. Strenuous exercise, such as hiking, will run the need higher.

Water Supply

Obviously no one can carry that much water, except by horse or motorized transport. In any desert trip, you should know where water sources are and carry as much water as possible. If a vehicle is used, a copious supply should be stored for emergency. Then, as we have pointed out, if a breakdown occurs you should stay with the vehicle to conserve energy.

Fortunately, over the major share of the land mass of this continent where emergencies may occur, water supply is not a great problem. The large forest tracts, the vast Canadian bush all have many lakes and streams. But having *pure* water may be a problem. Even high-country rivulets may be polluted, for example, by a dead animal lying in them. The old idea that water swiftly becomes pure as it runs a few yards in sunlight over a streambed is nonsense.

Happily, on trails in many State and National Forests water has been tested at springs or other sources and signs designate whether or not it is fit for drinking. But in an emergency you cannot count on finding one of those. Thus it is best to purify all water. Once a partner of mine got off his horse, drank deeply from a clear stream, and looked up to find a dead deer a few yards above in the creek. Especially in lower elevations, or in desert country where water may stand, purification is a must.

Purifying Water

Halazone tablets were mentioned earlier. Directions for use are given on the bottle. Iodine is also a purifier, with 2 to 4 drops per quart sufficient. Tablets used by the Armed Forces for water purification are available, too. There are other purifiers, such as chlorine, but those noted are easiest to carry and handiest for treating small amounts of water.

However, situations may arise where no chemical purification is possible—you have failed to go prepared, or have lost or used up the chemicals. Boiling water is the simple old wilderness standby. Many sources suggest boiling hard for at least five minutes. I'd suggest not being too eager. No harm is done by boiling twice as long, and even more to assure purity. Remember that altitude makes a big difference in how long it takes to bring water to a boil, and how hard it will boil with a given amount of fire.

Although water is seldom difficult to find in snow country, injury may make it necessary to stay put, or available water may be distant, and so snow must be used. If snow is plentiful, dig away the top layer, and use that underneath. It will be cleaner and more compact. A substantial amount of snow is required to melt down into a couple of quarts of water. If fuel for your fire is any problem, never fill a container brim full of packed snow and then begin to melt it. Melt a small amount and keep adding small amounts to the water formed. Melting will be faster this way. The same method applies if you must use ice. Chip it into small pieces.

Don't drink snow or ice water without boiling it. Each might be contaminated. Play it safe. It is imperative to stay well. Although boiled water will seem tasteless, some aeration occurs by pouring back and forth from one container to another. If you have foil, a second container can be fashioned from it. But emergencies are not comfort tours, and you may have only a single container. Drink the water flat and forget it.

A winter-camping, snowshoeing addict friend of mine carries a coil of small-diameter plastic tube for drinking from high-country streams when snow is deep. Granted, he takes in water that might be polluted, but under the snow mass that completely covers small creeks at high altitude the chance is slim. He uses the drinking tube because it is often very difficult to get down steep banks to the tiny open waterholes. Never eat snow or ice as a source of water unless it is absolutely necessary, and then only slowly. It may be polluted, and it chills your stomach.

Mountains and Forests

In the mountains of the North and in forests such as those of New England, southern Canada and the upper Great Lakes region finding water is seldom any problem. If you have a map, as you should, you can easily locate water, unless you are lost. If so, canyons, valleys, gorges, any "downhill country" all lead to water almost without fail. The water table in mountain valleys or in heavily forested northern regions is

Spring or
Seepage

Look for water seepages in the cracks of hard rock areas. Water creeps along the crevices, as shown in cross-section by arrows.

generally not far below the ground surface. If you do not immediately find lake or flowing stream, it is a good idea to know where water is most likely to occur and most easily acquired.

At the foot of any steep, broken rock wall where definite cracks exist in the rocks, running out to points, there are likely to be springs or seepages. Porous and soft rocks allow water to leach out easily. Hard rocks, such as granite, turn seepage along crevices. If you locate a mountain or north-country streambed that is dry but has bluffs and rock terraces rising above it, don't assume no water is present. Check the rock strata carefully. If there are hard folds above, then a layer of limestone or even sand or clay, look for green vegetation growing along the base of this layer. The entire layer may be filled with water. A small trench dug into the edge of such strata, right along where the green vegetation grows, may attract a quick seepage of water that offers an ample supply.

Dry mountain or northern-forest streambeds that show gravel can be deceptive, too. On occasion when you lie down and press your ear against such a gravel stretch you hear a trickle underneath. However, this

You may find water at the foot of a cliff which is broken into vertical columns. Also check around the bottom of a nearby pile of rocks.

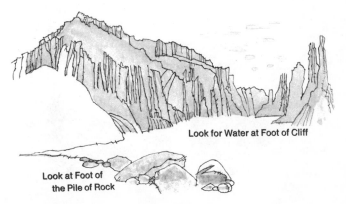

Look for Water at Foot of Cliff

Look at Foot of
the Pile of Rock

is a lucky exception and is by no means reliable. More often water is there and not heard. Dig a bit in a gravel bed, especially where the stream course is narrow. If the gravel continues on down a foot or more and is dry, better forget it. Remember that when you need water, energy spent digging deep holes is usually better spent seeking another source. However, if you strike *sand* beneath the layer of surface gravel, and it is damp, water may be nearby. Water sinks swiftly in gravel but not necessarily in sand. Damp sand may indicate that a foot or two down you will strike flowing water.

Don't ignore a dry river bed surrounded by bluffs and rock terraces. Investigate the outside of a bend carefully; a layer of limestone or green growth along the base means water is present.

Greener Vegetation, Dig Here

Sand

Clay

Water-Soaked Sand

Because clay soil retains water, check any damp spots of vegetation on a high clay bluff. Dig around the sand at the edges of a clay area, or even in the clay soil itself.

On my own property in the Texas hill country we have a creek that flows year-round. But in hot weather long stretches of it go underground. I've had people who I've taken down there sympathizing because my stream is dry. But a few rods on downstream there is a bubbling, gurgling flow bursting out of the gravel to flow over solid rock.

Often in mountain or forest country water can be found at unexpected locations. For example, an area of clay soil atop a high bluff is a fine water source. This is because clay soils retain water. In building earthen dams engineers often use clay for a core; it holds back the water. A damp spot atop a clay bluff may indicate a reservoir of water. Look closely at the edges of the clay area for sand, or any soil with lesser water-holding properties. A hole dug here, or even in the clay, might fill with good water.

Vegetation Clues

Vegetation growing in specific places offers excellent clues to water, in forested and mountain regions and in arid areas. A good plan, particularly if you have a binocular, is to scan the entire surrounding region, checking out both land contours and vegetation clues. Even though a water course is unseen, a line of brush that can be identified as alder or willow invariably means water. Tamaracks and balsams grow in low, wet places, and in the North cedar is associated with stream courses or lake shores.

Large willow trees always mean water, and because their root system is shallow but spreading, they commonly indicate water close to the surface. You do not need to find a stream or lake or bubbling spring. A cedar or tamarack bog or alder swamp will offer pools of water, stained from leaves and decaying vegetation but not necessarily impure. Boiling will make it potable, even though some taste—especially in cedar and tamarack swamps—may remain.

Arid Country

In severely canyon-cut, rocky country, scan very carefully the headers of short, sharp draws or canyons. These draws may be of solid rock, but with trees growing along the edges. You often find a flat place where clay or muck has accumulated over many years on top of the rock, where heavy water-oriented grasses or sedges grow. This is true of my area of Texas, and it occurs almost anywhere throughout the continent where such canyon terrain exists. Heavy grasses indicate that water has been here over many, many years, perhaps only seasonally. However, a hole dug into the thin clay or muck below such grasses often emits a seep of water.

In numerous arid locations a rocky bluff that overhangs an apparently dry streambed has ferns clinging to it at specific spots. This indicates porous rock and sure water. I have chipped out indentations in such porous overhangs and started a drop of clean, cool water on numerous occasions. This can be a lifesaver, with an almost unlimited supply of water to which a small clump of clinging ferns in an otherwise desert situation directed you.

Throughout vast expanses of arid country, across the plains and the desert, the cottonwood tree is a sure indicator of water. It is found along stream courses. Many will be dry or at least appear so. Look for *large* cottonwoods. An ancient one of large size indicates that a consistent source of water has been here for many years. Dozens of times a pool of water will be discovered in an otherwise dry wash near a cottonwood. Or, a bit of digging in the vicinity—try upstream first—will uncover seepage. Mesquites, however, growing along a wash usually mean little chance for water. Whitebrush thickets along a wash mean, in the Southwest, that water is near.

In any arid region, glassing or searching may turn up spots of outstanding green: at the base of a rock outcrop, in a low place along a wash, even part way up a rock terraced barren mountain. Especially lush patches of different vegetation are usually indicators of water. Getting to the water may not always be easy. Conversely, there may be a spring or small oasis lower down and wide open for your use. It is surprising how water plants—even cattails—colonize a small spot in desert surroundings where water is permanent. Undoubtedly seeds were transported by birds.

Bird and Animal Signs

Birds are very much worth watching. Flights of doves, common in U.S. deserts, all moving in the same

Flights of birds all moving in the same direction, especially in late afternoon or early evening, are likely to be headed for water.

direction toward evening or late afternoon mean a waterhole. Doves are extremely mobile, long-distance flyers, and may be going to a hole too distant for you to reach that day. Nonetheless, take a bearing on them, and watch them closely. Watch for quail, too. Some desert quails may get along fairly well for long periods without water, other than that taken from vegetation. But any desert area that *abounds* in quail will have water within 100 to 300 yards of such a concentration. Quail stay bunched up resting in shade during the middle of the day, but go to water early and late. Be particularly alert in desert situations for such birds as blackbirds, or water-oriented birds such as a few ducks in flight. Blackbirds are not desert creatures but are occasionally found in arid terrain, invariably near water. Any bird flights, regardless of species, that take a definite tack, are worth checking. They must have a water supply at flight's end.

Watch animals, too. I said earlier that following game trails when you are lost is usually a poor idea. But a game trail, or a convergence of several, may lead you to water. A very well worn mule deer trail in desert mountains, one that goes downhill, may well be a trail leading to water. Such trails are often seen from high points at great distances when you scan with a binocular. Watch desert mule deer with special concentration just prior to and at dawn. They have a habit of drinking *at dawn,* then going up into the rimrocks to bed down in shady crevices for the day. Don't expect to find a huge spring as their water source. They are desert creatures, getting along on what is available. It may be only a rocky depression that holds rainwater.

Caves or hollowed out places in rock bluffs may contain water. But be cautious about entering caves, because of snakes and the chance of getting lost. If you note a cave or hole in a rock wall, even one you cannot reach, watch it closely at evening. If swarms of bats emerge, remember that they are mammals and must have water. They will usually head for water right away. Their course may give you a clue.

Desert Hints

Again let me caution against any vast amount of digging for water in desert terrain. The amount of energy used up may be too much, or it may be expended to better advantage in other ways. For example, following a definite, time-worn dry stream course in a desert, not just a flood wash, not only may lead in due time to a larger, live stream, but it may also bring you to small pools among rocks or in gravel and sand, even in hot weather. Evaluate carefully "sure" indications of water. For instance, in such a dry streambed, the *outside* of a bend is the place to check most meticulously. If the bank is concave, and a depression exists, water has stood here. Sandy loam should at least be probed here. If it shows any dampness, on surface or a foot down, then digging is worthwhile.

If you are outfitted with quality maps of the desert region where you are going, you should check beforehand all indications of springs and other water sources. Invariably they are shown on the maps. Then if you are not lost but have a breakdown on your hands, you can study your map and determine precisely where a water supply is located. Another type of arid-country water source nowadays is seldom mentioned. Finding it requires knowing where you are, and having its location or locations exactly pinpointed on your map. Over a number of years game management people have been building, often in remote desert expanses, what are known as "guzzlers." These are water traps, designed to catch, hold, and protect rainwater over long periods, for use by game birds and animals. Some have been built in desert bighorn sheep country, to make possible spread of range. Others are for desert quail and deer. They are designed so that these creatures can drink but cannot get into the water and thus pollute it. Contact game department personnel for locations of guzzlers in the "outback" when planning a trip as a good precaution. Mark them on your map.

Plant Sources

Vegetation is a water source in emergency. There is hardly a place where you have much difficulty finding water across the northern half of this continent, but the arid areas are problem locations. Fortunately it is here that water-conserving plants, such as the cacti, grow most abundantly. The barrel cactus is always cited as a desert water source. It is a good one, too, but it does not grow in all desert locations. If you hack off the top of this cactus and slice and hack the pulp inside into pieces, a substantial amount of juice, mostly water, will accumulate. Prickly pear is the most common cactus and comes in great variety. The pads and fruit both contain large quantities of juice. The problem in handling cacti as a water source is the danger of getting scratches or cuts from spines,

To get water from a barrel cactus, hack off the top and crush the pulp inside to pieces until a substantial amount of water accumulates.

which quickly fester. Beware the fuzz in small clumps on prickly pear fruits or pads, or on any cactus. The various prickly pears and flat-pad cactus species are, incidentally, excellent food items as well as water sources.

With the exception of the coconut, beware of plant juices that are milky. Among desert plants, stalks of mescal, sotol, and Spanish bayonet all can be cut and drained of their juices for emergency water. In jungles, or even some shaded desert locations, varied vines are found. When you are tapping any of these for water, reach up as high as you can to cut first. Then cut the section at the bottom. The juice drains downward when the two cuts are made, but the top one must be made first to keep sap from rising. Green coconuts contain milk easy to get to. But the chances of getting into a survival situation in green-coconut country on this continent are rare.

In fact, the water-from-plants idea has been highly over-popularized. Even "cactus water" is not the bub-

Juice drained from vines in jungle or shaded desert locations can serve as emergency water. Two cuts, at top and bottom, will start the juice flowing, but make sure to make the top cut first to keep the sap from rising.

bling fountain it is sometimes pictured to be. I have camped among prickly pear, thousands of acres of it, during dry spells when you couldn't have coaxed a quart of water from fifty pounds of pads. They contract and grow "thin" during dry times. The common grapevine is one of the most overworked plants of all in popular survival literature. Large wild grapevines are an excellent source of juice to substitute for water. Cut a length and drain the water into a container or directly into your mouth. But wild grapes seldom grow in severely arid expanses. In my travels over forty years I have *never* seen wild grapevines in any spot where I could not find water elsewhere within a short distance!

While it is important to know such sources of emergency liquids, or cordage, a false sense of security is possible. For example I read recently some advice about gathering wild grapevines to bind a raft together for a swift northern mountain stream in winter. There is just one drawback: at that latitude and in such terrain the chance of finding a wild grapevine is about as remote as finding a green coconut! Also liquid from vines—the wild grape is one—does not flow readily at all times. Summer produces best, winter not at all. In other words, know what is *possible*, but don't let cozy campfire chatter confuse the facts.

Seacoasts

It is conceivable (though not possible in many places on this continent) that you might be caught in an emergency along a seacoast. Along all northern coasts there is little chance of being far from fresh-water sources: streams which enter the bays or oceans, near-shore ponds and lakes, or inland swamps. But you might find yourself in sand dune country. It is possible, but again not surefire, that you will be able to get fresh water by digging in sand, not deeply, during low tide just at the highwater line on the

In sand dune country, look for fresh water in the first depression behind the dune closest to the sea. Dig a hole during low tide; stop digging when you hit wet sand. The first water in the hole should be fresh.

sand. In theory, the first water to come into a hole here will be fresh. It is less dense (lighter) than salt water. Or, at times you can go back among dunes and dig and locate seeping fresh water the same way. *But,* too many people accept this as a system that is *going to work,* and it may not work at all. Fresh water must be present. It's that simple. If it isn't, you don't get any.

Some distance back from the shore, perhaps among dunes but in the lowest spot, so a kind of seepage basin is formed, chances are better that if you get water at all, it will be partly fresh. It may be brackish. But a small amount of salt is not harmful. Filtering through thicknesses of cloth, or through sand, may help some. In no case should you drink saltwater. It can kill you, taken in any quantity.

Filtering Desert Water

Inland in deserts occasionally alkali water is all that can be located. It is hardly drinkable as is, but can be made so if not too severely alkaline. First filter it through sand. Do this by filling a cloth, even your shirt, with sand and pouring the water through it. But use sub-surface sand. Surface sand may be alkali-loaded already. Next boil it, but meanwhile place in the pot some charcoal or ash from wood previously charred in your fire. If you find desert waterholes, incidentally, with no vegetation at all growing around them, at least no vegetation which is alive, beware. This water probably is not drinkable, having leached out from the soil certain minerals that have literally poisoned it.

In deserts especially, conserving the liquids in your body is almost like finding water. Conserve energy during the heat, so you perspire as little as possible. Always keep well covered—head, arms, entire body— rather than removing your clothing. This may not be comfortable, but perspiration evaporates more slowly when you are clothed, and you avoid sunburn, which raises body temperature and hastens evaporation.

Ground Sources

In some instances dew is a source of water. In the desert, where temperature changes are wide between night and day, heavy dews may occur. A downed plane or a broken-down vehicle offers large surfaces on which dew can collect. Clean such surfaces as best you can. Prepare to mop up dew at dawn, squeezing out mop cloth into a container. A sheet of plastic, numerous

Don't let rain water get away. You can make a "run-off" from the split half of a straight pole with a V-notch gouged along the center. Use rocks to support the trough, which angles slightly downhill.

smooth rocks laid out at night, a canvas ground cloth or tarp—all can be utilized as dew collectors. Dew may even be utilized from vegetation. But small surfaces unfortunately do not furnish much. You must be up before dawn in order to collect as much as possible.

Plain mud can be a water source. Wallow absorbent material such as cloth in it, and squeeze out the saturation. Obviously this is impure liquid. It must be boiled. But a fair sized mudhole, mopped up, could save your life. Meanwhile, be ever watchful of the weather. At the least sign of rain, don't travel if you are in dire need of water. Begin immediately to arrange for catching all the rain water you can. Some ideas are as follows. Scoop a broad, shallow hole in the earth, lay your plastic sheet or tarp in it. Any small board or tree trunk or even a stick can work, in a heavy rain, as a "run-off" to direct water into any makeshift container. Make containers, in desperation, from broad leaves, or packed earth, or flat rocks.

If there is a dry wash near you that is narrow enough, you may be able before a hard rain to push sand and rocks into a makeshift dam that will hold back a flood of water long enough for you to get your share. Use every possible and available container, even to spreading your shirt, with sand spread atop it, inside a shallow depression. If a tree is near, tie a cloth around it and let a "tail" serve as a wick to drain water during a rain off into any type of container. Wring out the cloth periodically.

Palm trees are mentioned in all survival manuals. Many North Americans may be gulled into believing that they should keep an eye out for them. Palm trees are a clue to nearby, immediate, water, and to liquids from various types of palm-borne fruit. The trouble is that only far down in tropical North America are there palm trees worthy of mention in isolated situations that could possibly be helpful to persons who need them. In southern Mexico and Central America they are present. The sap from cut fronds or flower stalks might be helpful. But not within the continental United States and only in restricted areas far south of the border where these trees are *indigenous*. This popular fallacy instills confidence where it is not due. Palmettos, however, in the Southeastern low country, can give up water when fronds or stems or hearts are cut. But chances of need in this region are so few that only the fundamental knowledge is necessary. Other water is readily available, as in the Everglades, one of the few remote areas in that region.

There are many ways to filter mud and other sediment out of water. In cactus country, slash pads (as of prickly pear) and pour muddy water on them in a lined hole or container. The gelatinous moisture within the pads gathers the mud or sediment. Let muddy water stand overnight to settle out mud. Filtering through cloth, grass, a cone-shaped contrivance made from tough sedge grasses or reeds, or through sand, will help. None of these operations is especially important, *if you boil the water*. Mud is not harmful as such. Settle it out, then skim off the water and boil to purify, assuming you have no chemical treatment.

Survival 'Still'

Among the most important water-gathering knowledge is how to build a "still" to force water from what appears to be dry ground. Over the past few years the still made with a plastic sheet has been used a good many times for gathering much needed water. This is an important reason for carrying the plastic in the first place. Some exertion is required. In moderate temperatures this won't matter. In high temperature of a desert locale, wait until dusk or pre-dawn to do the work. To make a still, dig a hole at least one and one-half to two feet deep and a yard or a bit more across at the top. This depression should be bowl shaped. At the bottom, dead center, place a container, hopefully one with a reasonably wide mouth such as a boiling pot, or a container shaped from foil.

Now spread the plastic sheet across the top of the hole, and gently push down in the center so that it becomes a large cone with the apex directly over and within about three inches of the container. The sheet must now be tightly sealed around the rim of the depression by piling on earth dug from the hole, or rocks. When that is done, place a small weight such as a stone on the bottom, center, to keep the plastic snug and the inverted apex precisely above the container. This plastic cone, heated by the sun, will pull from the earth any moisture that is there. It is distilled onto the underside of the plastic and runs down to drip into the container. This is not absolutely infallible, however. There must first be moisture present.

A survival still draws out whatever water is present in the earth. To make it, you need a sheet of plastic and any makeshift container. Dig a bowl-shaped hole, 1½ to 2 feet deep. Place the container at bottom center. Next spread the sheet across the top of the hole, making sure it is tightly sealed around the rim with piles of rocks, soil. When the plastic is lowered in the center so it takes on a cone shape, put a small rock in the center to hold the point of the sheet directly over the container. When possible, line the hole with moisture-producers, such as the chunks of cactus on the left.

Variations add to the amount of water. If cactus is plentiful, hack up chunks and line the entire bottom of the hole with pulp before spreading the plastic and sealing it. The cactus will be dehydrated and the resultant water distilled and dripped into the container. If you have a coil of small plastic tubing, mentioned a few paragraphs back, lay one end into the container and bring the tube up the side of the hole and from under the edge of the sheet. You are thus able to drink without disturbing your still. This can collect a quart of water a day and under optimum conditions more.

No doubt other water-gathering ideas can be concocted. However, using the foregoing as a guide, you will be basically prepared. As in every other survival endeavor, good sense, calm approaches and reasoning are of the utmost importance.

8 / Food for Survival

THE FOOD WE are talking about here is wild food which can sustain you through wilderness emergencies. Not long ago I read a series of recipes allegedly for survival usage. One described a stew to be made out of any wild game you could kill. The directions explained how to treat the meat and finally said, "Now add your vegetables." Just where the vegetables were to come from, the author didn't say. True, you might have in your pack, as has been suggested, some concentrated, dried or dehydrated foods suitable for making a stew. It is also possible to make a rather good stew from a rabbit, let's say, and certain "wilderness vegetables." But the chances of having all the ingredients in hand at the same time are remote.

Thus, in this chapter foods and food preparation are treated from a primitive viewpoint.

Finding Meat

If you have a weapon, you probably can acquire meat. Almost any small animals, from rabbits and raccoons to armadillos and muskrats, and all birds, are good to eat. No person in a survival situation need worry unduly about game laws. With a .22, mentioned earlier as a survival weapon, in your pack, you can kill small animals and birds, even a deer. Shots at deer or other large game must, however, be at short range, and in the ear or head. Never waste ammunition, and never shoot at running animals. In very shallow water you can shoot and stun fish with a .22 or other rifle, at close range. Do not be fooled into trying to do this with a shotgun. It won't work once in a dozen tries!

The kill of a large animal, such as a deer or a javelina, will furnish meat for several persons or for several days if you must stay in one place. In high mountain country a deer will not spoil if skinned and hung where the dry air gets to it. If you must be on the move, you might bone out backstraps of a deer and some haunch meat and carry it with you.

An animal call stuck into a pack, whether for a one-day trip or longer, is a good little survival tool to complement the rifle or pistol. Raccoons will come to them. So will bobcats and other predators. Believe it or not, bobcat is not bad eating. I have yet to try fox or coyote, however! But a call, a small flashlight for night calling, which is most likely to be successful, and a .22 may garner some meat for you. Another weapon that will collect small game, if you practice beforehand to become proficient, is the slingshot. It is not a bad idea to have one in a pack, with a modest amount of regular ammo for it. You can also use pebbles. In case of a breakdown or crash, you may be able to scrounge material, such as elastic cord from a parachute pack and a piece of stiff cloth or rubber, and by cutting a forked stick put together a slingshot that will work at least on small creatures.

If you have no firearm, you can kill certain mammals with a long stick, club, or stone. The armadillo is not difficult to catch in your hands, or strike with a club. The porcupine is notoriously easy to approach and kill with a club. This creature has figured in many survival instructions. Porcupines are only sometimes present, however, and not easy to find. Surprising as it may seem, if you stalk javelina into the wind you can often get within mere feet of them, close enough to club and kill one with a rock.

Look for signs of raccoons, opossums, rabbits and squirrels in hollow logs, hollow trees, and stumps. It is exceedingly difficult to trap a squirrel in any fashion in a hollow. But I have caught cottontails in hollow logs by carefully blocking one end and using a long pole in the other. Long-furred animals such as the opossum and raccoon can be hauled out of hollows by use of a forked stick. The fork must be very strong, and short—one and one-half inch prongs —and the handle long enough to reach the animal. The animal must be where it can go no farther. The stick is jammed hard against it, into the fur, and twisted. Hide and fur both twist onto the fork and the animal is hauled out. This system works only under ideal circumstances. I have accomplished it several times, and failed at it also. Be ready with a club if you haul out a raccoon. These are awesomely strong, hard-fighting animals. A 'possum is dull and usually fairly docile.

Occasionally animals can be smoked out. This was long practiced by hillbilly 'coon and 'possum hunters until made illegal. You can build a smudge fire at the base of a hollow tree so the smoke is drawn into the opening. Sometimes burrowing animals can be driven out by pouring water down the burrow, and standing ready with a club as they emerge. Make certain there are not several burrow entrances and exits, and if so, plug all but the one. However, so few animals are burrowers that this is not likely to bring any vast return in meat.

Some official survival manuals suggest using fire—grasslands, for example, set afire—to drive out birds and animals. This is an exceedingly questionable practice. You might catch yourself in your own trap, or start a fire that burns out of control. From a standpoint of practicality, the odds against your killing something as it flees are awesome. To be sure, some birds or animals may be burned to death and can be located after the fire is out. But the man desperate enough to try this method of food-gathering is already too weak to profit much by it. I never recommend it. There are far better and far more efficient methods.

A *small* fire may at times be useful. For example,

pack rats commonly build huge nests in such places as cactus clumps. A fire set in such a nest has little danger of spreading and drives numerous rats out. Chances are quite good of killing one or more with a club. They are big, usually fat, and though not appealing as food, they are livesavers in some circumstances.

Snowshoe hares never hole up but live out their lives above ground. They can often be approached, especially when they are plentiful, at close range. They sit hunched in a form, thinking themselves hidden. Carry a long pole when approaching them. Move very slowly. Proper maneuvering might allow you to hit one on the head. Jack rabbits in brushy areas often have several forms scattered over a small area. Ease up to a jack and it will hop away to another form. Check exactly where these are. A jack does not want to leave its home bailiwick. There are individual differences among animals: watch closely the reaction of a single jack. If it seems less wild than others, keep following it, form to form, very cautiously, speaking quietly. I've used this technique often in photography. When after a while the jack tires of moving it will let you come within five or six feet. A rock or thrown stick will collect such an animal.

Snares and Traps

You can take some birds without weapons. During the summer moult, when ducks are nesting, there are several weeks when they are flightless. You can run them down in marshes and catch them by hand. Nesting Canada geese often stand their ground to fight an intruder and are easily killed. The big mountain grouse of the North, the blue grouse, and also the Franklin's or spruce grouse, another northern-forest bird, are exceedingly naive. Occasionally so are ptarmigan, the grouse of the far North, and young sage grouse. You can hit them with stick or stone. In some cases ruffed grouse that have never associated with man are also just as naive.

Ruffed grouse, ptarmigan, and sage grouse are usually approached on the ground. Blue and spruce grouse are seen perching as a rule. A good many have been caught, in emergency, as follows. If you have copper wire, or nylon fishing line—anything with which to make a noose that will stay open—secure a

> To catch gamebirds or small animals, tie a length of wire or string with a slip noose in it to the end of a long, slender pole.

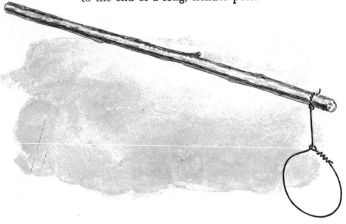

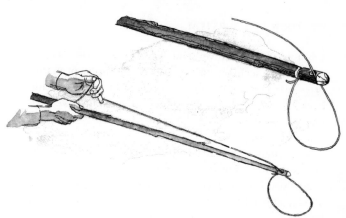

To make the more secure catchpole noose, tie
a length of rope to a notch at the end of a pole.
Draw the rope through a large screweye near
the tip of the pole, and bring it back to your
hands at the far end.

length with a slip noose tied in it to the end of a
long, slender pole. Reach with extreme care and slow
motion near a grouse and slip the noose over its head,
then jerk.

You can make a better noose arrangment on a pole
if you have ample material by arranging it like a
catchpole used in handling animals. In its "domestic"
form, a rope is secured to the end of a long pole, then
run back through a large screweye or other similar
holder set into the end of the pole, and the rope
brought back along the pole to the hands. Thus the
loop, slipped over the head of the animal, is jerked
tight by hand at the far end of the pole, and held
that way. This can be done primitively by selecting
the slender pole with care, then gouging a small hole
through it near the tip, or burning one through with

151

a hot nail or whatever you have. The noose material is now tied securely to the end of the pole, preferably in a notch cut for the purpose, and then threaded back through the hole, edges of which have been smoothed. A bird can be noosed more quickly and securely this way.

The noose, in varied forms, is one of the oldest "meat-getters" known to man. If you are in a spot where you can observe shore birds, wading water birds or waterfowl resting in an exact area—a sandy point, let's say, with cattails nearby—and you have enough snare material, make several nooses and lay them out where returning birds are almost certain to step into them. Then hide immobile in the cattails and wait. When a bird is in position, yank the noose tight. Sometimes a few small sticks laid parallel with the noose atop them to keep it off the ground will get better results, noosing a bird higher on the leg.

Birds such as lakeshore scavengers, the gulls for example, are caught now and then by burying a fish-hook, or a piece of bone to which a nylon fish line has been tied at center, inside a dead fish. The gull swallows the hook, or bone gorge, as it eats. Also, a small dead fish with spiny fins can be laid out as bait to catch a gull. Simply tie the line around the middle of the fish, or around the tail. The gull will swallow the fish head first. When the line is pulled snug, the gull cannot regurgitate the fish because of the dorsal and anal fin spines. Cruel, perhaps, but forgivable in emergency.

Let me urge you not to waste time trying to catch such birds as the waders (herons), the shorebirds (curlew, snipe, yellowlegs, etc.) or the fish-eating ducks (mergansers) by putting out fish-baited hooks. Herons and mergansers take only live fish. Shorebirds take few fish at all, but subsist on a variety of small mollusks, varied aquatic worms, and small shoreside crustaceans. I have experimented, twice, under simulated survival conditions, with attempting to catch these birds in this manner. It won't work. A tethered *live* fish in a shallows, however, will catch a heron, a merganser, or a

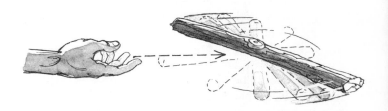

The best way to use a stick for taking birds is to hurl it with a spinning motion into the flock.

tern or gull. The best way to take shorebirds is to fashion a throwing stick at least two feet long, and make a careful sneak. They habitually consort in close-knit flocks, are rather naive, and with a bit of luck you can knock one over either on shore or in the air by throwing the spinning stick into the flock.

In the far North in summer, and in parts of Mexico in fall and winter, sandhill cranes gather by tens of thousands. These large birds are excellent eating. They roost standing in shallow lakes or ponds, gathered very compactly. If you stumble upon such a roosting site, wait until the birds come in at dusk. Mark a group well and at full dark wade very carefully out with your throwing stick. If you have a flashlight, this is easy. If not you must listen closely. The birds will "talk" most of the night. When close, hurl the spinning stick among the tight-packed flock and you may gather a fine meal.

Going back to the noose, the varied set snares utilizing it are excellent for meat-gathering attempts, for several can be placed and tended later. The easiest and most common animals for snaring are the various rabbits and hares. Well-used trails should be selected for the sets. Disturb the surroundings as little as possible, although rabbits do not shy from man scent, as most other animals will. Your repertoire of snares and makeshift traps should be small. It is better to become adept at two or three than to confuse the issue with dozens. Noose material is mandatory. Fine wire, which I have recommended for the pack, is good. Nylon fish line of heavy test is also useful. In dire emergency any cordage scrounged from clothing or a crashed plane or broken-down vehicle must serve. But be aware that at best the makeshifts are not likely to be very successful. The noose should be inconspicuous, and must slide easily.

To make the simplest of all snares, thrust two stakes down into the ground firmly, one on either side of a narrow trail such as a rabbit trail. At proper height, depending on whether jack rabbits or cottontails are likely to use the trail, bind a crosspiece to the stakes. Eighteen-inch height is a good average. If prongs from crotches are left on the stakes so the crosspiece is sup-

A simple snare across a narrow trail starts with two stakes driven firmly into the ground. Attach a crosspiece, supported by crotches on the stakes when possible, and tie the noose material to the center.

ported a bit, so much the better. The wire or other noose material is tied to the center of the crosspiece, with the loop dangling below at proper height so a hare or rabbit will run its head through as it moves along the trail. It may be necessary to keep the noose open, if limp material, by propping a twig or two near it. As the animal thrusts against it, the noose snugs down; the struggle keeps it that way.

The twitch-up snare is a variation. There are many ways to make triggers for these. The set is made as follows: Bend a springy sapling in an arc over the small game trail, or else bring its top down near one side of the trail. Drive a small stake, with a notch as in a tent

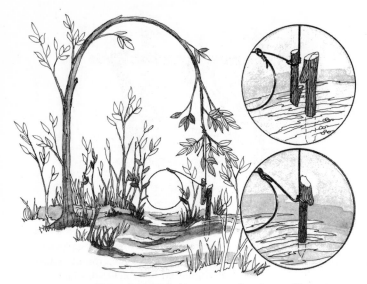

To make a twitch-up snare, bend a sapling over the trail and drive a notched stake into the ground where the top of the sapling comes down. Tie another notched stick to the top of the sapling, upside down, so when both notches are fitted together the tree remains bent. Tie the noose to the sapling end and drape it between bushes in the center of a game trail. For a simple variation, use a single forked stick (bottom insert) thrust into the ground and attached to the sapling to keep it lightly in place.

stake, into the ground exactly where the top comes down. To the end of the sapling top, tie a similar notched stick, upside down. Thus, when notch is fitted into notch, the sapling is delicately held in bent position. The noose material is tied to the sapling end and run out to be looped between small bushes at either side of the trail. Remember that a noose must be at proper height, and large enough for the head to slip through easily, but not the body. When a rabbit or other animal hits this noose, struggle instantly releases the hold of the notched triggers and the sapling yanks the animal into the air.

A much quicker, simpler method is to forget the notched trigger sticks. Use a forked stick thrust into the ground across the upper part of the bent sapling to hold it in place, but only precariously. The least struggle pulls it loose and up goes the snared creature. If the weather is severely cold, these traps may not work well, for the sapling may remain bent without spring. Incidentally, if you have wire strong enough, it is sometimes possible to snare a deer along a well-used trail. But its struggles are mighty and the snare must be very strong. It can be secured to a "drag," which is simply a hunk of log. This allows the animal to move some distance, and while it will invariably become entangled, the "give" may save a broken snare.

Noose snares can be set across the hollow of a tree base, or across a burrow mouth. However, with the exception of cottontails and prairie dogs, few animals but skunks, badgers, coyotes, foxes live in burrows. In other words, in most situations gathering mammals, and birds, without a gun is no snap, with the possible exception of rabbits. It is better to be aware of this than bitterly disappointed.

You can make an old-fashioned deadfall when no snare-making material is at hand. The classic is the ancient "Figure Four." I made many of these as a boy, trying them out on rabbits and even on mink and muskrats. The length of sticks used for the triggering mechanism depends on size of animal. For rabbits or hares, the stake that goes into the ground may be as long as eighteen inches. It must be strong. About four inches from the bottom a deep, flat-bottomed notch is cut into this stake. The stick that lies horizontally in this notch is slightly shorter than the ground stake. It is sharpened on one side. The other end has a notch deeply cut into its upper side on a slight angle (toward the stick end) so the notch has an overhanging inside lip. The trigger stick is about the same length. Its bottom is whittled flat and will fit into the above notch. At the other end of the trigger stick, two or three inches back from the end, a similar type of notch is cut.

A "figure-4" group of notched sticks holds up the log in a deadfall arrangement. The trap collapses when the animal nibbles at bait stuck on the pointed stake directly beneath the log.

Shove the stake into the ground. Place bait on the sharpened end of the horizontal stick, and lay it into the ground stake notch, with its own notch lying upward. The trigger stick now is hooked atop the ground stake and its butt fitted into the cross-piece stick. A heavy log is very delicately leaned from an acute angle and balanced atop this "Figure Four" mechanism—atop the end of the trigger stick. The log must be directly over the bait, and have the shortest possible distance to fall. When an animal nibbles the bait, the log falls to pin and crush it.

This primitive deadfall works well. The perplexing drawback in emergencies is—bait. For muskrats on a lake shore, cattail root may work. In fruit season, any wild fruit secured to the bait stick may collect anything from a rabbit to a raccoon. But often getting bait that will attract hares and rabbits is not easy. Occasionally a beaver is attracted to poplar or willow shoots tied to the trigger. If you have killed any creature, save the entrails and use them as deadfall bait for a predator.

You can build a simple box trap which is just a lidless box turned upside down and propped up on one end by a small stake, with bait under the box. Run a string or line to a hidden watcher. When quail or other birds or small animals are underneath, pull the string to jerk the stake free. In most instances, be warned, materials are not at hand to build a box, nor is it easy to find bait appealing enough to bring in the birds or animals. Also, from my many experiments with box traps and with the far better net wire traps, I can assure you that most birds and animals are extremely shy of them even when they are well-baited. Quail are not too difficult, if grain is available and you allow them to get used to feeding under the trap. But again, in a wilderness situation the grain is harder to come by than the quail and efforts may better be directed elsewhere. Desert quail are more easily snared with set nooses near waterholes or along tiny, brushy trails they utilize. If you have twine, you can weave a makeshift bird net to be draped in willow brush where ptarmigan abound, and which will also entangle quail along their runways. Again, expect failures to be numerous. If by chance you have a gill net as an emergency item in your pack, use it, draped in proper spots, to entangle birds.

Easy Food Sources

Many animal foods are more easily collected. During nesting season for birds, all colonial nesters offer opportunity for gathering eggs and sometimes young. Eggs are not harmful even when with partial embryos. Although this may not sound appealing, food value in emergency is high. Wild pigeons and doves, such as the Mexican red-billed pigeon and the whitewing dove of the desert, offer chances for a survival meal. Once deep in the jungles of eastern Mexico, had we been forced we could have made numerous meals from fat red-billed pigeon squabs. Their nests covered acres of low thornbrush. Along seacoasts the various terns and gulls also are colonial nesters. In the far North you can gather waterfowl eggs in quantity in spring, and catch young, flightless birds.

Frogs are a fine food source, found along streams, around lakes, ponds and marshes, and even in wet wild meadows. We have often gathered them to eat. At one backwoods lake my boys and I took sixty-odd in a couple of hours, stalking them carefully and armed only with sticks. Turtles also are fairly easy to gather. Any turtle is edible. Beware of their jaws! Throughout the Southwest lizards are common, and edible. None excepting the Gila monster of New Mexico and Arizona and parts of Mexico has a poisonous bite. These big lizards, though edible, are exceedingly rare. Lizards can be killed with a stick, although it is not always easy. They're quick.

With the exception of sea snakes, all snakes are edible. I've tried them several times. A big rattlesnake, bull snake, or water snake makes an excellent meal. And the club is the only weapon you need. If you've never prepared a snake, it is easy. Tie a thong behind the head (if poisonous, be cautious) and hang from a limb. Cut skin around below thong, slit clear down the belly, and pull it off. Gut the snake, lop off head and tail. It can be fried, boiled, broiled. The meat, if you can forget aversion to it, is excellent.

Crayfish, found in streams and under large and small rocks in shallows of many lakes, are a real delicacy. Certain northern lakes and southern rivers have them by thousands. Crabs are found along seacoasts and all are edible. You can catch shallow-water crabs with a piece of meat or dead fish tied to a string. The easiest method is to patrol the surf line or shallow bays at dusk or after dark, with a torch. Scoop them up with a makeshift net made from a shirt, for example, secured to a green stick bent to form a bow and handle. Or, skewer them with a sharpened stake.

Innumerable species of edible mollusks live along saltwater coasts. Various clams of delicious varieties are common along wilderness coasts of the Northwest. Search at low tide for their siphon holes. Inlets and bay shores near the sea also support mollusks. Don't always look for large ones. The tiny coquina, about half an inch long, a bivalve that looks like a miniature clam, is found on southeastern and Gulf beaches in wet surfline sand often by millions. Gather these, boil several quarts of them, then strain the shells and sand out through cloth. The broth is excellent.

In fresh water from North to South the common mollusk is the mussel or "freshwater clam." It lives in slow streams, and in lakes and ponds. Sandy or mud bottoms are the places to look. Often you can see their shells or the trails where they have moved about. There are several varieties, all edible. In some areas terrestrial snails are abundant. They, too, can be eaten.

All crustaceans (crayfish, crabs) and all mollusks (salt, fresh, or terrestrial) should be boiled. Do not eat them raw, for they may contain parasites. Freshwater mussels or clams are invariably tough, but offer substantial food value. The tails of crayfish are the edible part. If you have never cleaned crabs, remember that the body contains more meat than the claws. It's just harder to get out.

In severe situations, don't overlook the fact that insects can be eaten. Grubs found in rotten logs or under tree bark, grasshoppers, even termites are edible. It is best not to eat any of these raw, for they too may contain parasites. Frying them, if you have a speck of grease for the job, is the most palatable way, although they can also be boiled.

Cooking Meat

You should know how to cook meat in a primitive manner. Possibilities may be very limited. If you have packed as instructed, you will have salt. You may or may not have some dehydrated foods, but we will assume you have only meat and salt. This is no hardship. You can even do without the salt, but it is foolish to be without. If you have some sort of container, such as a basic go-light mess kit, the quickest, easiest method is to cut meat into small pieces and boil it. Use as little water as possible, to concentrate the juices. Do not put salt in the water. Conserve your salt supply. Boiling meat is the best way to assure that it will be cooked all the way through, if you give it enough time.

You can spear the pieces with your knife, or with a sharpened stick. Salt each piece as you eat. If you are in desperate straits for food, save the broth or cooking water. You can drink it, salted a bit, to give you strength. If you are not that needful, leave the broth in the container overnight: grease will be hardened in a layer on top the next morning. Wild meat may not have much fat, but there may be some. Skim it off and carry it with you, even if you must wrap it in foil or leave it in the container. It can be used later to help fry something, or to season a boiled wild vegetable!

Small birds or pieces of larger ones are easily broiled on a green stick over a fire or a bed of coals. They need plenty of attention while cooking, and you must turn them frequently. For a large bird like a grouse, run a green stick through it endwise, and lay this across crotched green sticks that have been thrust into the ground on either side of the fire. The bird must be turned; hold it in position after each turning by bracing another green stick against it. Without basting with some oil—which you undoubtedly don't have—upland birds are usually very dry, and may become hard outside, half raw inside. If you can spend the time, broil or roast them gently, high over coals for several hours. Or, wrap them in foil if you have it, double, and cook in the coals. This keeps all the juice and fats in. Waterfowl and shore birds usually have more fat. Don't skin birds; pluck them so the fat stays put.

Birds can be boiled, too. Conversely, slices of meat from a large animal can be broiled or roasted on a stick over a fire. If you must rush the cooking, make the slices thin. Where rocks, especially some flat ones, are handy, build a fire inside a ring of rocks, then lay a flat, clean one across the top. Slices of meat of any kind can be fried without grease on the rock. If you boiled meat previously and kept the grease, use it on the rock "skillet." I didn't say this is delicious, but it will sustain you!

Fishing Gear

In most emergency situations when you are without a firearm, fish may be easier to acquire than game. Hopefully you will have line, hooks, and split shot in your pack, and will have taken my advice about spoons and perhaps about a backpack rod-and-reel outfit. In much of Canada the "jackfish" or pike is a standby in lakes and slow streams. Spoons will get you all you can eat. With a hook and a scrounged bait such as worm, beetle, or minnow caught in a rivulet by hand, you might try for a small fish, then bait a larger hook with that one and catch a pike. In trout streams, and others, crawfish and aquatic nymphs are found beneath rocks. These are prime bait. Many a tiny creek holds wonderful meals of small trout. The farther from civilization you are, the more abundant the fish are likely to be and the more naive about taking bait or small spoon.

We must assume, however, that you may not have any fishing tackle. Take stock of what metal you have available from which a hook can be made—a safety pin is ideal; a needle or straight pin can be carefully bent, although the needle is likely to break. You can fashion wire into hooks. If thorny shrubs (such as mesquite) are in the vicinity, the stiff thorns, whittled off with a piece of wood attached, can serve as a hook. You can chip shells and bone into hook shape. However, hooks made thus, as Indians made them, require long, meticulous hours of work. Any hook made from pin, thorn, etc., has no barb. Thus when a fish bites you must pull instantly and keep pressure snug or the hook will slip out.

Because in most emergencies you cannot spend tedious hours of labor making a hook, the ancient "gorge" is the best and most practical solution. It can be made for any size fish, from a whittled piece of hardwood, a piece of shell, or bone. Basically, using wood, you can make it as follows: Cut a notch around a piece of hardwood perhaps one or two inches long, exactly in the middle. Tie the line here. Sharpen each end of the piece till very fine, and taper down from the center. With line affixed, thrust this gorge inside a chunk of bait—a crawfish, a small fish, or if the gorge is very small and intended for small-mouthed species, worms. Let it down and leave the line limp. Allow a fish which takes the bait to swallow the gorge. A quick yank jerks

Makeshift fishhooks can be whittled from wood, shells, bone. From left are a straight-line gorge, a U-gorge with thorns, and a wooden hook.

the gorge crosswise and the fish cannot get rid of it. The gorge dates back hundreds of years and when properly made is most simple and effective.

Another type of gorge can be made by cutting a short length of thorny vine, or a piece of shrub with thorns. Cut a slice with two thorns on it, and bend the piece in the middle to form a U, to which the line is attached. Let the fish swallow this. A hard pull sets both thorns. When no thorns are available, a carefully, finely whittled and smoothed section taken from the slender crotch of a hardwood branch can be fashioned into a hook that has the larger side notched and bound to the line.

Two types of spears were used successfully by many Indian tribes. Each is made from a green sapling, each basically in the same manner. The wood should be hard. Cut a pole several feet long. Split one end for

A fishing spear with toothed jaws snaps shut over a trapped fish. Use a wedge to keep the wood split while you cut sharp notches; remove the wedge and tie the upper end of the split when through. Finally, insert a strong twig to hold the jaws open until the fish knocks it away.

about seven or eight inches up the shaft. Force a temporary wedge into the upper end of the split, and cut sharp teeth or notches into each flat side of the split. For a trap-type spear leave them like this. Now remove the wedge. Bark or twine or whatever cordage is at hand is used to securely bind the upper end of the split so it will not split farther. Open the "jaws" and prop them open with a twig strong enough to hold them. When you jam this trap spear down over a fish, the twig is knocked out of the way and the jaws snap shut, holding the quarry.

For more surefire variation (the trap jaws may be inhibited from closing because they strike the bottom), whittle each jaw into a hard, pointed spear, with the notches cut very keen and sharp. Insert a permanent wedge and put on the binding. The jaws are not wedged as far apart as for the trap spear. This one is strictly for impaling a fish. Indians sometimes used basswood bark for the binding and covered and secured it with pitch. Used at night with a torch while carefully wading shallows, this spear can be very effective. If it breaks, another is quickly fashioned.

If you have hooks and lines with you, a good plan is to make set lines to leave overnight. These are exactly what modern catfish enthusiasts call "tree lines." Bait hooks and attach them to a tree limb hanging over water. When a fish is on it cannot break loose for the limb bends, playing it as on a rod. This will not work with thorn hooks that have no barb. But for catfish and other rough species it may work when you use a well-turned gorge. There is practically no end to the makeshift spearing devices you can concoct. A sharp piece of bone, a sliver of flint, a shell, or a pocket knife can be lashed to a pole. An impaled fish must be pinned to the bottom, however, else it will get away. By no means take a chance on losing your knife that way!

Various hard cane and bamboo make good hooks and spears, but chances of finding these in any wilderness on this continent are rather slim. With luck you might fashion a hook and makeshift barb, by using a section cut from shrub with long thorn, and then lashing in a notch another thorn, so that it points downward and just inside the point of the other. The line is attached just above the lashed-on thorn. When a fish bites, it is impaled on the thorn used as the hook, but the one lashed on above keeps the fish from slipping off.

Bait is seldom hard to find: terrestrial insects, aquatic nymphs under stones in creeks or in mud of lakeshore bottom, crayfish, worms, a small frog or minnow trapped in shallows and scooped up in cooking container. If you must fish through the ice, cut a hole and fish *on bottom,* using very *small* baits. Fish take smaller baits in winter because their metabolism is slowed. Make a primitive ice-fishing lure used for hundreds of years as follows, if you have no bait: Use a bare fish hook, or an improvised hook of hardwood, thorn or safety pin. Try to find a small, shiny piece of shell and work a small hole through one side, to fashion a small lure. A small piece of metal will do. The makeshift lure, with a few bits of thread or streamers of bark or piece of your shirttail added, is let down to bottom and jigged up and down so it twirls and gyrates. The second a fish strikes you must keep a steady, swift pull and flop it up atop the ice, or it will get off (if your hook is barbless).

If ice is clear and fish are in exceedingly shallow water where you can see them, you might be able to stun several by hurling a heavy rock or log into the ice above them, then smashing open a hole and collecting them. The chance of success, however, is very slim. I've tried it. The fish usually take fright and leave before you get near enough or before the rock strikes. And, except in extremely shallow water, where they are unlikely to be in winter, it is impossible to exert enough force with such a blow. But in a shallow pond it may be worth a try.

Making a crude fishing line, if you have none, is possible, though it takes patience. My advice is to try first to unravel strong threads from some item of clothing, or if absolutely necessary from a tarp or groundcloth. Then braid and twist the threads together to form a line. In making any line (of bark fibers also), always start with several strands of uneven length, and keep adding as one runs out. This assures that at no point will there be a weak spot where all fibers end at once and are spliced.

You can make a line by cutting thin strips from your plastic sheet and twisting them. Bark fiber lines, though crude and large in diameter and frightening to some fish, can be turned out fairly easily. Some tree barks or rootlets make better cordage than others. It is important to know these, but you will have to make do with what is available. Linden and basswood inner bark, mulberry inner bark and roots, hickory bark, elm bark and roots, and the root fibers from hemlock, tamarack and spruce are all good. Roots, however, are not as useful in emergency because they must be dug up. Try inner bark strands first.

Weave a line by carefully separating fine bark strands. Pounding strips of bark with a rock, or soaking them will help separate the strands. Using three strands (I've mentioned unequal length) secured to some object, hold one strand in one hand, two in the other.

Twist the single strand, rolling it between thumb and forefinger, *away* from the other two, until it is twisted tight. Now bring it across and over the other two, and take the next strand in line and twist it, and so on. As the shortest strand begins to run out, lay another beside it and twist them together and continue. The result, if you stay with it, is a primitive line as long as you wish to make it. On occasion when good fibers are available, simple braiding works well. (Larger ropes and cordage for binding rafts, etc., can be made in the same manner, using larger strands. See section on making a raft Chapter 6.)

You can make a crude net from a bow and handle formed out of a limber sapling, with a piece of clothing —shirt, underwear, or whatever cloth or netting is available—secured over it. Hordes of minnows commonly gather in eddies in small streams, or along lake shores. You can scoop them up with such a primitive dip net. Use them for bait, or cook and eat them. Don't attempt to clean them. Cook entrails and all. Larger

For an improvised fishing net, bend a sapling into a loop, and tie string to the loop in overhand knots.

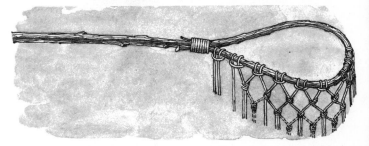

A rock-pool trap built close to bank or shore attracts fish you can scoop out with a net.

Build a more complex trap by driving stakes side-by-side into a river bottom. Fencelike walls extend out from the entrance, which is placed to let the current flow in.

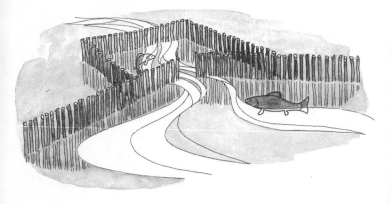

fish can be flipped ashore or netted from stream pools, or tidal pools. But muddy the water first or you'll have difficulty. You must scoop blind in muddy water, but at least the fish can't see to dodge. Fish hiding in vegetation or under rocks can be driven out, if two work together, after the water is muddied. The net is held just below, downstream, and the vegetation disturbed or rocks kicked.

Under optimum conditions, trap fish or drive them into a pool that is dammed with rocks or logs or earth; then slip them out with a makeshift scoop net. It is not impossible to build, from stakes placed close together, a fish trap, and then drive fish into it. Keep in mind that this requires an immense amount of work and may not be worth energy expended.

Cooking Fish

Primitive fish cookery is much like that for game. Cook small fish quickly as follows: Take out entrails and gills, but leave the heads on. Run a small, sharpened green stick into the mouth, on through the open body cavity, and into the tail section where the vent has been removed. Prop several such sticks with fish above coals and in five to ten minutes they are ready to eat. Assuming you have salt as I've admonished, you have a really delightful meal.

Larger fish should be split down the middle and laid open on a grill made by drawing green, limber wood such as willow switches into a kind of racquet shape, securing tip to middle with a bit of copper wire from your pack, then binding on crisscross pieces of green

To prepare fish for cooking: Clean it from the ventral side by cutting first with the point of the knife inside the mouth (1). Cut through the narrow strip of gristle joining gills to the head. Make the second cut behind the gill (2) to sever the membrane, between the bony ridge and the body, and continue the cut to the tip of the lower jaw. Do this on both sides. The third cut (3) severs the strip of gristle connecting bone and tongue. Finish by cutting from the jaw, along belly line, to the anal orifice (4). Hook your finger through the bottom of the gill cut, around the tongue, and pull sharply. The tongue, gills and intestines will come out through the belly slit. Run your thumb along the backbone to clean blood from the back vein; wash and wipe dry.

You can clean from the dorsal side by placing the knife tip ahead of the gill line until it hits bone. Cut along both sides of the dorsal fin, keeping as close to spines as possible. Spread slit with one hand to expose joinings of ribs to backbone. Make the same first three cuts as above, but don't cut along the belly. After the ribs are cut, remove gills from the slit on the back. Spread the fish to remove backbone and dorsal fin.

Large fish cook more easily on a simple grill. Make one by bending a switch into racquet shape, and attach green willow pieces in a crisscross design.

willow (or facsimile) to make the grid or grill. This can be propped above coals, or balanced on rocks above coals. Cross-cut steaks of a large fish, or fillets with the skin on, can be "fried" on a hot rock, fillets skin-side down. The trouts and salmons especially are oily and furnish at least enough of their own grease. Such fish wrapped in foil and cooked in or on coals will be fine for the same reason. As with game meat, a quick and efficient method for fish is to *boil* them, if you have a container.

Don't discard heads, fins or tails when boiling fish. Cut up the fish and toss it all in the pot except gills and entrails. (Save those for bait!) This is the way fish stock is made in any seafood restaurant. It is highly nourishing. If you will be staying put for several days, or even a day, the stock (any game stock, too) may be utilized as a base in which to boil various wild plants.

Some books describe gimmicky methods for cooking game and fish, such as plastering birds, feathers and all, in mud and burying them in coals. Or building a fire in a pit, wrapping and burying meat, and covering it with dirt for some hours. These work, the latter delectably. But they are tricks. During emergencies the easiest, quickest ways to nourishment are the best. They save on energy and time. Either or both may be important, depending on whether you are traveling or waiting it out, and on your physical condition.

Foil, which takes up little room, a spool of copper wire, salt, a container for boiling, and your knife are about all you need for primitive, emergency cooking of game and fish. On short treks I have even put into the rucksack a good-sized tin can. Other items can be stowed inside it to economize on room. The can becomes a coffee or tea boiling pot, a meat pot, etc. With just a tin can and a supply of salt, plus your knife, you are in the survival business in pretty good shape.

Remember that whether you are eating meat or fish or the in-betweens such as frogs, crawfish, or turtles, and adding certain wild plants to this scrounged-off-the-country diet, there may be some stomach upsets. An abrupt change to survival diet should be avoided if possible. In other words, if you do have some food supply you are used to, intermingle the "new" foods as slowly and sensibly as you can while you "taper off" from civilization.

Edible Plants

There are literally hundreds of edible wild fruits, nuts, plants and roots. The problem with them as related to survival is their vast numbers. Most outdoorsmen know or learn to recognize a standard few, but it takes a great deal of study, both in books and in field identification to be sure of large numbers.

Recreationists should make it a point to be able to recognize the available edible vegetation in the areas they utilize most of the time. For example, a sportsman who hunts and fishes in Minnesota should certainly know the edible plants and fruits of his state that are most easily found in emergencies. He should know what time of year is best for each: young shoots, fruits, roots. In addition, the outdoorsman who is going to a new area should research the plants and fruits there. You should at least be able to identify the most abundant and common ones, which may become vital resources if you are lost or otherwise in difficulty.

There are dozens of good library volumes which contain complete material. In many states the game and fish departments or the university can help with information about wild edibles in their location. You can never amass too much knowledge, that's sure. But my approach here, a sound one for the average person, is to cover the wide variety of possibilities throughout the entire continent, and conclude with examples of species *easily recognizable* and *most abundant over large ranges.*

Fruits. Let us begin with fruits. Wild fruits are found in every state and province. But in any given locality most are available only at specific periods, which may not be prolonged. And fruits are usually abundant in spring and summer, with only a few in evidence in fall.

Wild red mulberry trees are found from Texas and across the South on up throughout the Ozarks and throughout New England. They are quite common in State and National Forests, especially in the South and the Ozarks. The very sweet fruit ripens in spring and early summer and falls fast. Serviceberry shrubs, in some areas spreading small trees, are called "shadbush" in the East and various names westward. They are

Red Mulberry

Wild Raspberry

widely distributed throughout most of the U.S. and Canada. Their white blooms come in early spring, before the leaves. This is a summer fruit often abundant in wild locations, especially in old open burns or lumbered areas and along streams.

Wild blackberries, wild raspberries, wild dewberries are found over a tremendous range, one or more in any locale of the U.S. and Canada. Vast patches of wild blackberries occur, for example, in the Great Lakes forest region. Red raspberries are profuse over much of Canada and also in Alaska. Dewberries, low-growing and vinelike are predominantly southern. These are all summer fruits, with August an average ripening time in much of their range. Delicious wild strawberries range over most of temperate North America, in mountains and forests where there is shade and quite often in grassy locations. They ripen in summer.

Blueberry   Huckleberry

The blueberries and their cousins the huckleberries both include several species and grow on bushes from a few inches to several feet tall. They are possibly the most abundant and important wild fruits of "emergency areas" throughout the northern states and Canada and some distance down the eastern U.S. mountains. Open woods, burns, and logged regions offer them by untold acres, usually in late summer and into very early fall.

Prickly Pear   Elderberry

The foregoing are the most widespread and abundant of the fruits. There are many others. Cactus fruits, such as prickly pear apples when ripe, are delicious and sustaining, but watch the hairlike spines. Elderberries are not especially palatable but widely distributed and worth knowing. Bearberry or kinnikinic is a mealy berry chiefly of the northern wild areas that has some food value. Wild rose hips (fruits) are most important because they are found even in winter. Wild northern gooseberries make good eating but are scattered and never plentiful. The highbush cranberry of the northern U.S. and parts of Canada is edible after frosts, though not especially desirable except in jellies. However, you should know this one, a prime ruffed grouse food. The pawpaw and persimmon are edible but not likely to be important in wilderness emergencies, although an ability to identify them can be helpful.

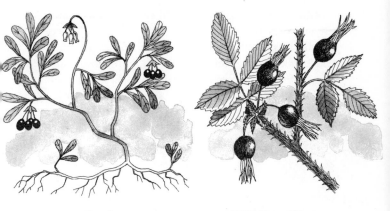

Bearberry

Wild Rose Hips

American Papaw

Persimmon

Wild bog cranberries and wild currants are possibles, but not very important. Wild cherries, chokecherries, pin cherries, sand cherries on low vinelike bushes, and wild black cherries on big trees are exceedingly abundant, especially across the northern U.S. The problem with them is their "puckery" taste. They contain sus-

Wild Cherry   Chokecherry

taining sugar but may cause intestinal upsets. Wild black cherries or the rarer sand cherries are the best of the lot. Wild grapes may be locally important because they range widely across much of the U.S. and some portions of southern Canada, and especially as they sometimes hang on the vine from late summer into fall. Wild plums are an important fruit of broad range, particularly in late summer and early fall, but the majority of plum thickets are in areas close to civilization.

The major problem with wild fruits, and wild plants, is that you must also know what *not* to eat. The simple method, and listen closely, is to know a major share of the *wholly edible varieties* which are in the majority, and not be tempted by anything you can't absolutely identify. You might get a wee bit of nourishment, or

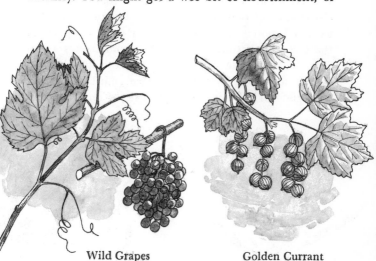

Wild Grapes   Golden Currant

wind up defunct, by guessing. Search for *what you know*. Beware of *what you don't know*. For example, some fruits are poisonous raw but not if cooked. Others, some common, are poisonous, period. Examples: blue cohosh; bittersweet; chinaberry; mistletoe; nightshade. In many treatises on wild fruit the May apple is noted as delicious. It is, but other parts of the plant are poisonous, and even when the fruit is fully ripe it is on the "caution" list. So are wild holly berries, pokeberries, Solomon's seal. Thus, eat only berries that are commonly known, abundant and easily identified.

Mushrooms. All live-off-the-country experts agree that emergency people should leave mushrooms alone. Species like the spring-growing morels are delicious. But no mushrooms contain much of food value, and the chance of poisoning is too great. Our family has gathered morels for years in widely scattered parts of the U.S. But I would never recommend this as a survival measure. We happen to know the morels well. Others may not. Besides, as stated, mushrooms just taste good. They give you very little, if any, "steam."

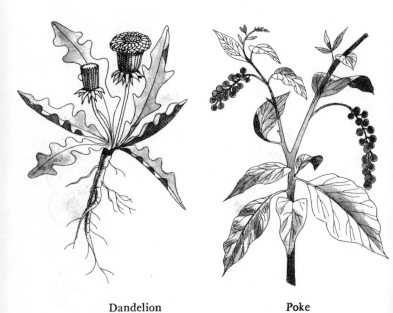

Dandelion   Poke

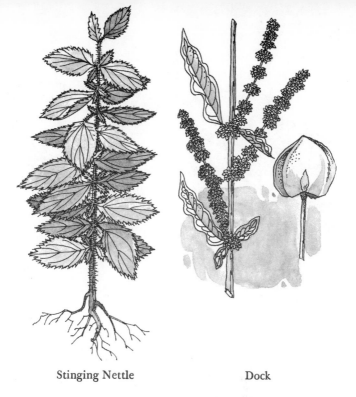

Stinging Nettle   Dock

Plants. Next come edible green plants. Their numbers are vast. Many make rather tasty boiled greens. Probably the most wide-ranging of these is the dandelion. Young plants are less bitter than mature ones. A quick scalding in boiling water, then draining and final boiling, removes most of the bitterness. Various clovers, found throughout most of the U.S. and commonly in woodland openings or thin shade, are next in line as easy-to-find. Clovers may persist in sheltered locations well into frost time. The entire plant, including root, is edible. Boiling is the simplest preparation.

Other plants found over most of the temperate continent that furnish edible greens are nettles, several

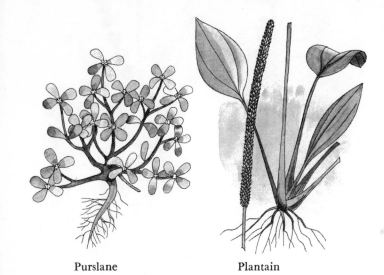

Purslane

Plantain

Burdock

varieties of dock, purslane, plantain, and even pigweed. Burdock, also common over much of the northern U.S. and southern Canada, can be used for greens. Young leaves and shoots are best. Stalks, peeled and salted, are not bad, and if you learn to identify the first-year stalks of this perennial (which lack flowers or burrs) you can peel and cook the roots. Mustard, found in great fields throughout wild lands across the northern U.S. and across into Canada, is easy to identify and makes a palatable dish. Even the flowers can be cooked.

Two favorites of mine that we often eat as a wild treat are watercress and marsh marigold. The latter we called "cowslips" when I was a youngster. Both these plants range over much of the continent. You can find them in wet openings and along streams. Since stream

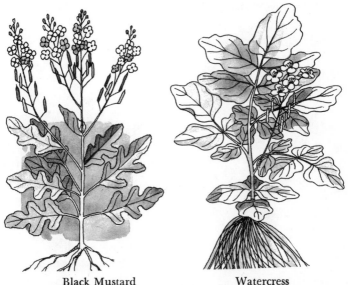

Black Mustard   Watercress

courses are highways to many outdoorsmen in emergency, these plants rate high as survival food. Neither grows in every moist terrain, but one or the other are almost certain to be seen somewhere. Spring and early summer offer the best greens from marsh marigolds, when leaves are young. The same is true of watercress, but watercress is often found quite edible all through the season until total freeze-up. It can be eaten raw and usually is. But it also makes fine greens. A piece of boiled, salted meat with watercress greens is a good wilderness meal.

Wild celery ranges widely and can be used raw or boiled. The shoots of young bracken, the large tough fern of Canadian and U.S. woodlands that often grows in profusion, make a good dish in spring when the "fiddlehead" shaped shoots are edible. Fireweed is an-

Marsh Marigold (Cowslip)

Bracken

Lichens (Reindeer Moss)   Lichens (Rock Tripe)

other common plant found over a vast range, growing
at its best in burns, logged-over areas, and other openings. The stems should be boiled.

Cacti. In the Southwest and some other desert areas,
there is a wealth of food—and drink—in various cacti.
Although these should be handled with extreme care,
the pads of the abundant prickly pear when peeled and
diced are excellent. Diced cactus is commonly sold in
Mexico as a green vegetable to be boiled. Mexicans
living far out in their deserts hack off the great blooms
of the big yuccas and boil the flowers as a vegetable.
Mesquite beans, green or ripe, can also be utilized for
food.

The list over the continent is virtually endless. Even
grass of almost any variety can serve for greens. And in
the North you can boil the nutritious lichens. Know
how to identify the most common edible fruits and
plants. And try to study thoroughly beforehand the
entire vegetation picture of a wilderness area *where
you are going.*

Roots and nuts. There are a number of roots, tubers, nuts and grains to add to the list. Most common and far-ranging is the cattail. Young cattail shoots in spring

Cattail (Elephant Grass)   Arrowhead

make a good boiled vegetable or can be salted and eaten raw. A bit later when the green flower heads appear, you can boil them and eat the outer layer. In the fall or even in winter, if you have means to keep dry wading after them or a good drying-out fire, dig the roots and boil them like potatoes. Arrowhead grows along pond and lake shores and along the edges of slow streams over most of the U.S. and portions of Canada. It has tuberous roots which can be gathered from late summer on into winter and boiled or roasted.

Spring Beauty   Jerusalem Artichoke

That common wildflower of damp woodland locations and stream courses, the spring beauty, has a small root tuber that is edible. Another that outdoorsmen should know, although its range is not as large, is the so-called Jerusalem artichoke. This tuber is available in autumn in portions of mid-Canada and the U.S. Sedges also have small, edible root tubers.

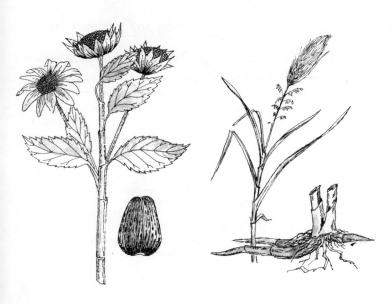

Sunflower Seeds   Wild Rice

Wild sunflower seeds make a good energy food but
are a bit difficult to husk. They are available in fall
and winter. So is delicious wild rice, throughout the
Great Lakes region, parts of eastern Canada and the
U.S. However, a canoe or boat is all but mandatory for
harvesting it. The most common nuts found over the
continent are, in the Northeast beechnuts, in the South
wild pecans, and in some locations both North and
South, black walnuts and hickory nuts. The prime and
most common nut of all in wilderness areas of the West
is the piñon, the small, delicious nut found numerously
in the cones of a species of pine. You can identify it
easily. During some falls piñon nuts are abundant;
other years there are very few. These must be rather

Beech Nut   Black Walnut

Hickory Nut   Piñon Nut

laboriously shelled, but you can gather a great many under or from a laden tree. They are most nutritious.

In dire circumstances, willow buds and shoots and even the inner bark layer, can stave off starvation. The inner layer of pine may also be cooked and eaten, or even eaten raw. Make a serious attempt to know wild foods. Try a few, using some primitive cooking methods when there is no emergency. Sometime try an overnight backpack during which you force yourself to live off the land. It is a valuable rehearsal for survival.

9 / Fire and Warmth

IF YOU HAVE OUTFITTED as suggested earlier—with water-proof matches, even with fire-starter tucked away in your pack—fires should be very little problem. Assuming you do have fire-making materials, there still are certain tips that will be helpful. For example, even if you are cold, don't be in a wild rush to get a blaze going. Whenever you build any fire, for warmth over-night or for cooking, get all the materials together in a proper place and be sure all is ready *before* the match is struck. Matches are infinitely valuable. Haste and poor preparation defeat your purpose and waste matches.

For a midday cooking fire, pick a sheltered location and make a very *small* fire. If it will be a fire for eve-ning cooking and for overnight, plan a larger one, or

several small ones *around* you. Without fail, select a
fire site that is *safe*, where a fire cannot get away from
you and into grass, leaves, needles. For overnight, build
where it cannot set your shelter ablaze. In the latter
case, choose your sleeping site *first* and build the fire
in relation to it. Don't build under evergreen boughs,
even if they are green, and especially if they are covered with snow.

Starting the Fire

Start any fire with patience. Plan it carefully and
one match will do. Get as much out of the wind as you
can. Lay a foundation of fine tinder such as birchbark
shredded into small pieces, or tiny dry dead twigs from
a conifer, or bits of dry willow. If necessary, whittle
shavings or cut fine shavings along the side of a stick

> A fuzz stick made from dead wood makes re-
> liable tinder. Whittle fine shavings along the
> side, leaving them attached to the stick.

Arrange your firemaking material by laying a foundation of fine tinder beside a short length of stick. Lean larger twigs above the tinder, against the stick, in a pyramid. Have larger wood, 3 to 4 inches thick, ready to add once the twigs catch. Light the tinder from the bottom, on the upwind side.

but leave them on the stick. This is called a "fuzz stick." Crisscross above the fine tinder a few larger dry *twigs*, but none more than pencil size to begin. Have increasingly larger wood at hand. A good method is to lay the tinder beside a short length of stick three to six inches in diameter, lean the twigs over the tinder and against the large stick. Now when the tinder catches, the twigs go in a moment, larger ones are carefully added, and in seconds a good blaze is there.

For overnight stays, don't stint on gathering wood. But save energy by burning long pieces a bit at a time, pushing them farther into the fire as they burn, rather than chopping or sawing. Always gather standing dead wood if you can, or at least dead wood not lying on damp ground. In wet situations, and I have experi-

An Indian fire built with logs radiating outward and a small tepee of sticks in the center
saves energy and fuel. Push the logs into the
fire as they burn.

enced this in desert as well as northern forests, gather
very small dead twigs from standing conifers or mesquite, not from the ground.

If you have a fire-starter, you have no problem. If
not, shelter a tepee of these tiny twigs and hold a
match diligently under it, or light and use your candle.
Be ready to add more. With patience you can get a fire
going even with damp twigs. Keep drying out larger
sticks as the blaze grows. Always light your fire with
the breeze at your *back,* and on the side nearest you,
and from *below* the tinder. Once you have a big fire
going, pile on damp or wet wood gingerly (not eagerly)
and let the fire dry it. You must use care not to smother
your blaze. Always leave space, but not too much, by
crisscrossing or leaning the sticks, for air to circulate
beneath to keep the fire going. Too much space lets a
fire die. Almost, but not quite, contact the sticks.

When possible use wood from conifers (evergreens) for starting fires. Dry cones are great, too. The hardwoods do not blaze as readily, but fires from those last longer. You may not have time or energy to go around selecting woods. Just remember that pine, cedar, spruce, etc., will start the fire quickly and burn swiftly, and woods such as ash, oak, maple will keep it going longest yet may be more difficult to start. Aspen, poplar and birch are common firewoods in many forests. They make good cooking fires, burn hot and fairly fast. Oak, and mesquite in deserts, make marvelous coals and long lasting fires, but are hard to ignite. On sagebrush plains, you may have to gather a lot of material, but sage burns readily even if damp, and makes a very hot but fast fire. Dead cactus woods, such as cholla or saguaro, are too hard and burn hot and slowly.

FIREWOOD RATING OF COMMON TREES

Good	Fair	Poor
Ash	Beech	Willow
Hickory	Mulberry	Alder
Oak	Buckeye	Chestnut
Holly	Sycamore	Magnolia
Dogwood	Tamarack	Tulip
Apple	Pine	Catalpa
Birch	Cedar	White elm
Maple	Juniper	Cherry
Locust	Spruce	
Mountain	Cottonwood	
mahogany	Fir	
	Aspen	

If tinder is a problem—it can be tremendously important—stay alert to possible sources as you travel. Pause to pocket some that looks good—a double handful of dry pine needles, a few cones from pine or other evergreen, a roll of birch bark, some dry cattail heads, a mouse or bird nest, or globs of pitch from conifers. In sparsely vegetated desert country, do the same with dry mesquite, sage twigs or bark shreds. Few North American deserts are so barren, that you will lack something to burn. In arid grazing country, dry cow-dung burns well.

It is to your advantage, except under desperate circumstances, to make a small fireplace to contain your blaze. A few rocks will do it, or a small hole scooped in sand. This keeps a fire in place and assists you in cooking. If the weather is extremely cold, keep your mittens or gloves on until you are all set. Many a blaze has been fumbled because of numbed hands. A friendly, large blaze is tempting at evening, but don't overdo it. Small, controllable fires fed progressively are best and safest, even if you must arrange several around you. Stay with your fire until it burns down to a good bed of coals. If you must have an overnight fire, don't have it blazing when you turn in.

Keeping It Going

A couple of good chunks of logs laid across the coals, with any rocks removed so the logs *touch* the coals, will hold a fire overnight. Lay them so that the rounded sides touch each other but not too snugly. The small blaze will come up between them, and heat from each keeps the other going. Properly laid, this keeps a gentle but warm, low fire all night, and by morning the logs will be barely burned in two or only partially so. Be absolutely sure, even under the strain of survival conditions, that your fire is dead-out when you leave it. I want to repeat here something mentioned earlier. From an overnight stop

When the ground is wet, lay a base of large logs and sticks, and light the fire atop them.

where you have had a good fire and found good conditions of shelter, available firewood and water, be sure you mark your next day's trail well. In case of some second difficulty, you may need to come back!

It is easy to keep a fire going when it must be built on ice, or snow, or wet ground. Melting is slow because the heat goes up. However, if you must build on snow, ice, or wet ground, if at all possible lay large logs or poles for a base and make your fire atop them.

On windy days, find a protected spot and build your fire there.

Think always in terms of using a fire to your best advantage. If a rock wall or small scoured-out indentation large enough for sleeping is present, and the wind is not blowing *toward* it, a fire laid so you will be between it and the rock makes a cozy spot. Try your best to find a fire spot, at least for overnight, out of the wind. Even small midday fires will be far more efficient, and save you much time, if built in a protected spot.

Before laying a fire, think carefully about what you have and what you need. If you need warmth all

Two green logs provide a fireplace for all-night warmth. The logs can also support a pot.

night, build a fire almost as long as you are, designed in a rectangle, with a green or partly green log on either side. You can build a backstop for a fire, out of rocks, or logs, to reflect the heat. Old hands often build a self-feeding reflecting fire if they are staying for some time. This is done by driving stakes into the

Build a backstop of logs to reflect heat through the night.

ground on a slant, and stacking logs one atop the other at the outside edge of the fire against these slanted stakes. As the bottom log begins to burn, it slowly lets another down. A backstop can be built simply to reflect heat into a tent or against a rock wall. If wood for backstop is dry, drench it or throw mud on it. However, this is a lot of work and may not be worth the effort in your particular case.

Cooking Fires

For a cooking fireplace, look for flat rocks to surround the fire, so you can set utensils upon them. Try to find a flat rock to reach *across,* for a skillet. A small fireplace or pit built with rocks laid in a "V"

Rocks arranged in a keyhole design make two fireplaces, one for warmth and one for cooking. Start the larger, warmth-giving fire first, at the end of the pit farthest upwind. Use coals from this fire for cooking at the other end.

or a "U," with the open end *toward* the breeze or air movement, will allow draft in that open end to help keep the fire going. If too strong a wind is blowing, reverse the open end.

An excellent technique for a fire for both warmth and cooking is to make a long pit or fireplace of rocks large enough to contain *two* fires. Build the large one at the end of the pit or enclosure *farthest upwind*. Add wood progressively until a good bed of coals is formed, with an ardent blaze atop. Now coals can be raked out with a stick and piled at the other end of the pit. These are for cooking. As more wood is added to the large warming fire, more coals are always ready. Cooking is done with heat of the large fire moving *away* from the cook, and the coals do a better, gentler cooking job than the large blaze.

The most important consideration in efficient fire-building is to start with very small, exceedingly dry and flammable bits and pieces. A man who is hurrying, who makes a tepee of small round branches each, say, half an inch in diameter, is going to have to start over. The same small branches, however, split into halves or better still quarters will ignite far more quickly. Think always of starting a *tiny* fire, and of having progressively larger material to add quickly. But the first and second additions should be of small size, and no large chunk should be added until the fire is blazing well.

Wet conditions. In rain or snow, firemaking becomes more important, and also more difficult. Remember that preparing properly to light the fire also becomes more important now. There is nowhere that a fire cannot somehow be started in rain or snow. These times, incidentally, are when that tinder picked up along the way and stuffed into a dry pocket will be tremendously important. Break open standing dry wood, or gather small twigs of evergreens back in under spreading branches. If a sheet of birch bark, or a flat rock that can be turned up with a dry side, is available, set up a shelter, even with your jacket propped by sticks and make your try for a fire under its protection. Now the old-fashioned fuzz stick, split from inside a piece of dead wood and shaved along one edge with your knife so many small shavings curl off, comes in handy. Get just a couple of shavings or twigs going on a dry base and then gently tend it until it starts to blaze.

Conserving Materials

Suppose your matches are at a premium. You might consider attempting to carry coals with you between stops. This was done in ancient times and is still done today in some primitive areas. For, make no mistake, starting fires without matches, though possible, is seldom quick and easy. The main caution in carrying coals is not to set fire to some of your belongings. Keep this in mind. The easiest way to carry coals is to use your cooking pot, or tin can. Coals left deep in ashes from an all-night fire will hold for hours, if little air gets to them. Place ashes in the bottom of the pot, coals on top, then more ashes. The lid cannot be placed on tightly. But with ample ashes covering coals, they will still be glowing by midday, even if in dire need you have to carry the pot in your hand as you travel. Do not use material that will blaze up. You can in a severe situation cut green bark and roll coals and ashes up in it, plugging the ends lightly with dry moss or punk (rotted wood).

Without Matches

There is always the chance that you will be in a serious situation without matches. The chief consideration is that though fire-making is certainly not easy, it is by no means impossible. After all, Indians and other primitives lit fires daily for many centuries before matches were invented! Knowing the various methods, utilizing whatever equipment you have, and infinite *patience,* are now your allies. Are you as smart as an ancient Indian? Be prepared for failures, but don't give up. If you are caught at night and in rainy weather but weather not seriously cold, make up your mind to suffer through the night and hope that dry weather comes in the morning. It is very difficult, without a flashlight and with everything wet, to get a fire going without matches, but in daylight you can check out every possibility.

If you have had a vehicle breakdown, or have been in a plane crash, probably some fire-starting items will be at hand. But if not, remember that the electrical system of vehicle or plane, if not totally destroyed, can be used to start a fire. If gasoline is available, tie a rag or anything that will soak up gasoline tightly around a stick and soak it in the gas. Unhook a spark-plug wire. If the ignition system will work, turn on the switch and work the starter, with the gas-soaked rag between plug and end of wire. Jumping sparks will ignite it. *But,* if you are alone you'll have to jump out and be quick to grab it. Better still, get sparks from battery terminals. This is easily done by crossing a wire from one terminal and tapping it against the other. Be sure the wire is insulated, however.

If you do not have electricity to work with, but gasoline (or oil) from plane or vehicle is available, it is equally valuable. If you must leave the scene and travel, find some sort of container and take some gasoline with you, even a pint. Without matches, a few drops placed on the tinder you'll use will catch a spark quickly. Some insect repellents are highly flammable. If you have some in your pack, these may help in starting a fire much as gasoline.

Regardless of how or where you find yourself without matches in a survival situation, first thing to do is take stock of what possibilities you have. Gasoline and insect repellent are handy. If you have a firearm, you may be able to start a fire by using a cartridge or two. But before you do this, see what else is available, and save your cartridges for a last resort. Also, be forewarned that though a large caliber rifle or a shotgun works fairly well, a .22 is at best marginal, for its cartridges do not contain enough powder or enough blast from the small primer. In addition, today's powders are slow-burning and regardless of caliber or gauge, starting a fire this way is difficult. Following, however, is the procedure.

Using a gun. First, gather the very best tinder you can find and get it in place. Have dry twigs and tiny shavings also ready. (This is basic for any fire-starting method.) Remove the bullet from a rifle cartridge by working it loose with your knife or tapping gently around the cartridge neck with a small stone. Have a small piece of cloth ready. It can be cut from your clothing or handkerchief—anything you have—but it should be thin, and if you fray the edges it will be all the better. Pour about half to two-thirds of the powder from the cartridge into the piece of cloth. If you are using a shotgun shell, cut away the crimp, pour out the pellets and remove the wadding; then use part of the powder. Be careful now to keep the shell upright so as not to spill the rest of the powder. Stuff the cloth with its powder very *loosely* into the gun *muzzle*. Load the shell or cartridge into the chamber. Keep the gun pointed straight up into the air. Stay beside your fire site, and shoot. The cloth, if all works properly, will fly a few feet into the air and fall back either afire or glowing and smouldering. Catch it instantly and place it upon the tinder. Blow on it if necessary, but be gentle. Add tiny twigs or shavings as you get a small flame.

Using a glass. Probably the easiest method of fire-starting without matches is by using a glass. I suggested earlier ("What You Need For Emergencies") that a small magnifying glass, and a binocular, should be in your pack. You may have one, or both, of these. Other glasses that can be used for fire starting are a camera lens, a watch crystal, a telescope sight lens. A piece of clear ice, shaved and shaped and melted in the hand to form a makeshift lens is a possibility, although a difficult one to use successfully.

Of course, making fire with a lens requires sunlight. You might have to wait on that. Bright sun is best,

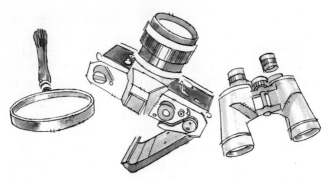

Fire without matches is possible if you have a magnifying glass, a camera, or a binocular lens. Catch a spot of sunlight on the glass, focus on the lower part of a pile of tinder laid below. To use the camera effectively, open the back, remove the film, set the shutter opening to the widest f-stop and focus sunlight through the front of the lens.

although occasionally weak sun will do the trick, given time. Lay out your tinder and other fire materials. Hold a magnifying glass a few inches from the tinder. Experiment with distance and tilt it so the bright, hot magnified spot of light is exactly on the *lower* part of the small pile of tinder. The focus here is used so that as it smoulders the heat will rise to ignite the tinder above. If the tinder is dry and highly flammable, and the sun bright, smoke should rise in no more than sixty seconds. If no flame appears, but smoke does, blow gently on the tinder, or fan it a bit, keeping the glass focused. In a few more seconds a flame should appear.

To use a camera for this, open or remove the back, take out the film, move the shutter opening to its widest f-stop, and set it so it will stay open. It can be held open by keeping the trip button depressed. Focus the sunlight through the front of the lens so that the hot spot is on the tinder. With a binocular, remove a lens and use it. Likewise with a telescope sight. A watch crystal works like a small magnifying glass. Two, with water in between, will work better, if available. If you wear glasses, the more the correction, the better a lens will work. The small magnifying glass does the best job with the least difficulty, and it should be a part of your gear, without fail.

Flint and Steel

The most common wilderness method of fire-making when this nation was young was striking sparks with flint and steel to tinder. In an earlier chapter I mentioned the Metal Match available nowadays. However, the back of a knife blade, an axe, or any piece of metal will work. You do not need actual *flint* rock, although it is renowned as a spark-maker. Quartz, agate, various pyrites and jasper are all good spark-making rocks. If in some desperate circumstance, you find yourself without any steel or iron object, you can usually discover along a stream bed or dry wash chunks of rock, that, struck together in a severe, down-stroking manner, will themselves strike sparks. The traditional combination has been a piece of flint (or other spark-making rock) struck by the back of a jackknife blade while the knife is closed.

Think of the flint-and-steel method as comparable to the way a cigarette lighter works. There is the piece of flint and the steel flicked against it. Or, if you have traveled in a recreational vehicle using a butane refrigerator, you know that a quick twist of the steel rod strikes a spark against flint that ignites the butane gas pilot light. But these ideal conditions are made almost foolproof because the *tinder,* in each instance, is a highly inflammable gas. It is therefore easy to understand that under primitive conditions the *tinder* is the most important part of the combination. It absolutely must be capable of catching a spark and allowing it to smoulder enough so it can be coaxed into flame.

Emergency tinder. This requires the best of all possible materials. It is said in some survival manuals that *charred cloth* is the best tinder because it catches easily and holds a spark. Pioneers often carried charred cloth just for this purpose. But where the person in a survival situation is supposed to get his piece of charred cloth, no one ever explains. Nonetheless you can take a tip from this. Let's say your match supply is dwindling. Make it a point to ignite a piece of cloth, perhaps after your fire is lighted; then when it burns briskly, smother the flame. Put this charred cloth into a small bottle, or a piece of foil—anywhere where it will be safe and dry—and keep it against the need for starting a fire with flint and steel.

Some tinders used by early Indians were dried puff balls (watch for these as you travel), rotted wood filled with fungus growth (it must be absolutely dry), and the dried pith from inside elderberry stems. The unraveled end of a rope may serve in a pinch. Likewise the lining from bird and mouse nests or the totally shredded and pulverized bark of cedar or birch or sage. If you can kill a bird for survival, save the finest feathers or down for tinder. An unraveled gauze bandage, if you have one, might do. Search your pockets for lint and collect it. Or unravel cotton threads. Or cut off some of your own hair. Lift dead bark and scrape dust and pulverized wood where worms have worked. If you know you will have to try making fire with a spark, gather all such bits of tinder and carry them with you. Guard them very carefully, keeping them totally dry and laying them out in sun to dry further when possible.

The spark, or shower of sparks, must fly right into the tinder. Place the tinder in a small pile on a dry surface, and, holding the rock and your knife above

Good materials for the flint-and-steel method are a jackknife struck against a spark-making rock, or steel against a piece of flint fastened to bottom of a waterproof match case. Strike with a sharp downward motion, cupping your hands close over the dry tinder and driving the sparks toward the center. When tinder starts to smolder, blow it gently into flame and add kindling gradually.

it, strike downward with the knife (or another rock) to drive the sparks home. Some experts hold the tinder in the palm of the left hand and the flint between fingers of that hand. This cups the tinder out of a draft, and when the steel strikes, the spark is sent into the tinder in the palm, where it is gently nursed and blown into flame. Then it is quickly placed in a cup of dead grass or other tiny kindling, and the fire is progressively built up. Remember that you are still far from a campfire, even though your tinder smoulders. Nurse it with all the care you can muster. But don't give up. You may try two hundred times and finally succeed. If you have carried a bit of gasoline from immobilized transport, use a bit on the tinder as an assist. Or, if you can spare a cartridge or shell, use some powder.

The basic problem for most people when they attempt to work without matches is that they are *trying for the first time*. What you should do is *practice* fire-making under the most primitive conditions right at home. The first thing you will learn is that it is extremely difficult. But you will also learn, with practice, how to do it. This assures that when you really need to make a fire in primitive fashion, you not only realize the difficulties, but also have confidence that perseverance will bring success.

Fire Drill

The flint-and-steel method, next to the magnifying glass method, probably gets the quickest results with the least amount of effort. Indians of various tribes used the bow-and-drill method effectively. Make no mistake, fire-making this way is difficult even under optimum conditions. But you should at least know how —and again, you should *try* it until you succeed, at home, so you will be informed and practiced when the need arises.

The principle of the fire drill is friction. A pointed stick (the drill) is twirled into a notch in a fireboard, grinding off fine powder. Heat from the friction of wood against wood causes the powder to smoulder as it drops through the notch onto tinder already placed there. Some woods are much better than others for this endeavor. Willow, various elms, basswood and cottonwood, and in the desert, wood from yucca are among the best and most common. Others among the conifers are tamarack, cypress in the south, cedar, and balsam. Others will work. But any of those mentioned, if available, should be first choices. And, the drill and the fireboard, remember, are always of the *same* wood. That is basic. These are high-friction woods and one piece worked against another generates heat best.

Various Indian tribes fashioned various types of drills, but in general the *fireboard* was about the same for all. This board must be split from a branch or log. If you have an axe, that is no problem. If you have a knife, it may be possible with patience to whittle wedges and then, with a rock for a hammer, split out a fireboard. Traditionally it is about an inch in thickness, though it can be a bit more or less. Width is not especially important, but at least three to six inches is convenient. And, the board must

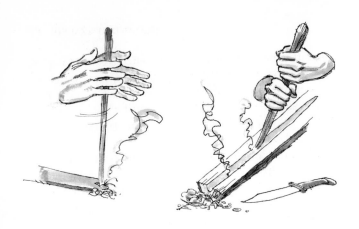

A fire drill is difficult to operate successfully, but when there are no other possibilities, it is worth a try. On the left, a tapered stick is twirled swiftly back and forth into a notch at the edge of the fireboard. The smoldering wood powder ground off drops through the hole onto the tinder below. On the right, the drill is drawn back and forth along the long V notch, driving the wood powder out at the bottom.

be long enough, at least a foot, so you can hold it down firmly by kneeling or with one foot.

If you have split out a board with bark on edges, cut it away and have one edge of the board as smooth and straight as possible. Now gouge out a hole in one side of the board, about an inch in from the edge, perhaps a bit less than that. This is the hole the drill will fit into, so first just get it placed properly and gouged possibly a quarter-inch down into the board. Now cut a V shaped notch in the edge of the board, the V pointing toward the gouged place and cutting into the edge of it. Bevel the notch so it is wider at the bottom than at the top. It is in this notch and below the edge of the drill hole that the tinder will be placed, and in which the powder, ground by friction, and ignited by the heat, will fall.

The simplest hand fire drill used by some western Indians was a slender rounded stick about one and one-half feet in length. It was smoothed as well as possible and its upper end was *tapered*. That is, the larger end fitted into the gouged hole in the board. To make one of these, keep fitting the end of the drill into the hole, forming the drill end so it fits and making the hole so that the twirling drill will rub all the way around except where the notch is in the edge of the board.

This "hand drill" is operated by kneeling on the end of the board, and placing the palms together around the upper, tapered top end of the drill. The palms then are "rubbed together," twirling the drill back and forth (reversing directions with each rub) and swiftly. Meanwhile pressure is put on by a downward thrust, and the palms quickly work downward. When near bottom the pressure is swiftly released, the palms brought back to the top, and a new start made. This requires practice to keep the operation smooth and constant. The powdered wood ground off and heated eventually sets off smouldering as it falls into the tinder, and you can nurse a blaze to life. Often a piece of bark or flat stone is set beneath the board and the tinder placed on it. Thus, when a spark catches, the tinder can be quickly removed and placed under the small twigs and more fine tinder previously laid close beside the fireboard.

Two persons can work this simple drill better than one. They should face each other. As you run your palms down the drill, your partner seizes it at the top and continues. This keeps it in constant motion and applies all possible pressure and constant friction.

Bow-and-drill. The bow-and-drill is more complicated, but more easily worked and perhaps more efficient. And, since pressure and speed are the essentials for creating fire by friction, this is undoubtedly the better method. The fireboard is fashioned in the same manner, the tinder placed the same. But the drill, to be most effective, is shaped somewhat differently. It can be as little as a foot long, and need not be smoothed and round. In fact, if it has several sides, six or eight, like some pencils, it will work more efficiently. The grinding end is rather bluntly tapered, to get the most friction in the hole. The upper end is more tapered, whittled down to a rather blunt but pointed end so the least friction will occur there.

The next item is the crown to hold the top of the drill. This can be a stone of palm size, rounded on top and with a hole in the bottom side, or it can be a piece of wood shaped roughly to the palm (like a tree burl) and with a hole for the top of the drill to fit into the bottom side, but not snugly. Your palm will put pressure on the drill by pressing down on this protective socket, but the drill must turn easily in it. If you have any kind of grease, or even candle wax, work it into the socket hole to help the easy twirl of the drill there.

Now the bow is made. It is simply a fairly stout piece of limb that is curved in bow shape. It should not be long enough to be unwieldy, but can be up to two feet. Try to cut the bow so there is a crotch at one end. Cut a notch around the other and attach the bow string securely there. You'll have to use whatever is available. A rawhide boot lace makes a good string. Or, if you have it, a length of nylon cord, or twine. Indians used a thong of buckskin.

The tension on the bow string must be exactly right. It can be adjusted, if you have selected a bow with a crotch at one end, simply by twisting the thong and hooking it with a loop in that end over the crotch. The idea is *not* to have the string tight. The drill is set into the fireboard hole. The bowstring is looped once around the drill about halfway down its length. A good position is to kneel, with the left foot solidly holding down the fireboard. The left hand palms the protective socket atop the drill. The bow, held in the right hand, is drawn rapidly back and forth in a sawing motion. The thong, looped around the drill, thus twirls the drill first one way and then the other. You may find it necessary to adjust tension on the thong, one way or the other.

It is obvious that the motion must be exceedingly vigorous and as fast as you can make it. Thus a stout bow and string are required, and plenty of pressure should be put on from above. To keep the drill steady, wrap your left arm around your left knee solidly. That is the foot that holds down the board. If you are lefthanded, reverse these directions.

Some Indians made more complicated drills. But any firemaker will have complications enough with those described. It is possible, though exceedingly dif-

HOW TO BUILD A FIRE
WITH BOW AND DRILL

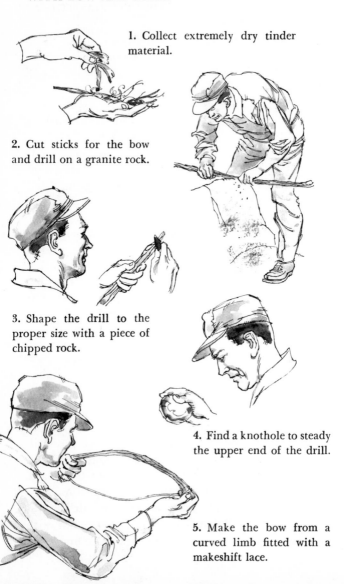

1. Collect extremely dry tinder material.

2. Cut sticks for the bow and drill on a granite rock.

3. Shape the drill to the proper size with a piece of chipped rock.

4. Find a knothole to steady the upper end of the drill.

5. Make the bow from a curved limb fitted with a makeshift lace.

6. Loop the slack in the lac around the drill, and place on end of the drill in the notch o a stick placed over the tinder with the knothole atop the dril to keep it steady, saw the bow rapidly back and forth, whirlin the drill in the notched stick

7. Blow on the tinder to help the spark catch.

8. Swing the tinder in the air to give it more oxygen.

9. Get a real campfire going by adding tinder gradually.

ficult, to get a smouldering wood powder by propping the end of a small, very dry log of good friction wood atop another and drawing a rope underneath. A notch should be cut into the bottom of the log to hold the rope steady. Tinder is laid exactly beneath the notch and the log is barely propped above it. One holds down the log with one foot, holds one end of the rope in either hand, and saws furiously back and forth. There are two reasons for low-rating this method, as against the others. A rope may not be at hand, and if one is it may be swiftly worn in two.

Fire saw. A "fire saw" can be fashioned by cutting a notch in a rounded stick of high-friction wood, then sawing a V-shaped piece at right angles back and forth in the notch. If the rounded piece is split in two, and one half hollowed out below the notch so powder is dropped into tinder placed in the hollow,

A fire saw is less effective than the drill, though it works on the same principle of friction. To obtain the wood powder, saw a V-shaped stick at right angles across a notch cut in a rounded stick of high-friction wood.

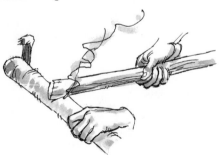

a fire may be contrived. Another method used by some pioneers and occasionally by Indians utilizes a fireboard and a stick like the drill. But in this instance a slot about a foot long is gouged out in the top of the fireboard. The end of the "drill" stick is placed in the notch. Pressure is applied with both hands and the stick furiously rubbed back and forth in the notch. The powder formed is eventually ignited, and transferred to tinder. This method is by no means as effective as the drill.

Practice

Don't wait until dire need arises to see if you can make a fire by these various methods. Try it at home! Practice makes it work smoothly. I do not want to sound too discouraging about these fire-without-matches methods, but it is unfair, and even dangerous to make it all seem very simple. It's far better to be warned that it is not. Remember, when the chips are down you won't be giving a Boy Scout demonstration with all the materials flawlessly made and every condition optimum. This may be for real!

One reason I urge you to try fire-making without matches at home is that by the time you've found out that it really can be done, you'll be so impressed with the difficulties that you'll never be caught without matches! Just remember that fire-making for comfort or cooking is easy anywhere on this continent, even fairly simple in the worst weather, if you have that finest and simplest of all fire-making friction devices—a dry match!

10 / *Shelter*

THERE ARE MANY varieties of emergency shelter. The type you utilize will depend upon the kind of emergency that has caught up with you, and *where* you are. In a hot desert location you will need shelter not for warmth, but for shade. In severe cold you need to get out of wind and keep as warm as possible. There are some situations in both hot and cold country where insects will be an anguish and shelter must be selected to fend them off. Insects usually mean mosquitoes.

Insect Protection

A smudge fire, started with dry material and with green grass or boughs added intermittently, will form smoke to help against insects. But the *location* of a camp and shelter will be most important. Try for a point that runs out into a lake, on the side where an inshore breeze blows. On a seacoast the dunes just in from the surf may be swarming with mosquitoes, but dry sand immediately above high-tide line will have a breeze that will keep them away. In mountain and swampy areas of the north, get up on a ridge to make your camp; avoid the low places. If you have taken insect repellent, the kind I've suggested, you will be in fair shape. It is not possible, however, to fashion a makeshift shelter that is completely insect-proof.

If a plane crash or a broken-down vehicle is the difficulty, here are some suggestions. The interior of plane or vehicle may protect you from insects, and ordinarily in places where they swarm the climate will be neither excessively hot nor excessively cold. However, in extreme cold or extreme heat, both plane and vehicle interior (if not smashed up) may be colder, or hotter, than a shelter you can fashion outside. A great deal depends on what you have with you for warmth or shade. Shade can be improvised under a plane wing or beside or under a vehicle out in the desert. Parachutes can be utilized in many ways. But in severe cold, consider that you may be able to stay warmer in a snow shelter, or one of snow and evergreen boughs, than inside plane or vehicle. Ordinarily you will be staying by the plane or car, not traveling, for this way you will be found more quickly.

Where To Start

The chance is very good in any of these break-downs that most of the materials you need, at least for a few days—food, etc.—will be on hand. And the chance is that you left word where you were going and will be found. Thus you can take time to make as comfortable primitive living quarters as the materials at hand will provide, improvising with chopped branches or leaned sticks through which such materials as cattails or willows are woven.

However, the man on the move, on his way out or lost and trying to get out, has an altogether different problem. In all likelihood he will use a shelter only one night at a time. He cannot take time to gather food, water, and firewood, cook food, boil water, make up his bed in a sheltered spot, and still have much time left to fashion more than the most primitive, most easily and quickly devised shelter. Next morning he is on his way again and the shelter is discarded.

Remember to stop traveling *early* enough so you can get your work done before it is dark. Base this on the type of terrain. If you must gather rocks or a lot of small switches, like willows, to make shelter, it will take longer by far than it will in dense forests of the mixed evergreen type.

Suppose you are traveling, lost or otherwise. If you have properly outfitted as suggested for a long trip, you will have shelter with you. In plane or vehicle difficulty this would be the case, in the event you deemed it necessary to walk out. If you have a full-fledged backpack outfit with a three- or four-pound tent and light bag, you have no worries about shelter. Even without a pack, if a light tent and bag are in the plane or vehicle, you can contrive lashings to pack them with you, and you certainly should. Or, if you must make a choice between tent and bag, make it in relation to *where* you are. In a desert you don't need the bag but the tent would be valuable. In cold weather, you can run up makeshift shelter and the bag is more valuable.

Tarp Shelters

Let's assume, however, that you find yourself in a situation where a plastic sheet or tarp is all you have. Or, you have one of these plus a light bag. It is invaluable to know how to fashion shelter quickly. Think in terms of very simple, primitive shelters. The beautifully planned, elaborate shelters often pictured for Boy Scout projects, for example, are really exercises in fun and games. They are of little practical value to a man in an emergency and a hurry. Only if you are *staying in one spot* should you spend long hours building elaborate shelter. In some cases it is good therapy, something to do even if unnecessary.

The tarp or sheet, plus a broken canoe or small boat—suppose you have found a canoe or small boat to use to float a river—can quickly become a crude shelter. Tilt the craft on its side, leaning at an angle so there is space beneath. It must be safely propped in this position. Secure the tarp at the rail, or by

Tarp serves as a shelter in many situations. On a canoe trip, stretch it over a tilted canoe and stay dry during the night.

A bough bed is a buffer between you and the cold. Insert branches in the ground, facing the tips in the same direction. Space the rows six inches apart and cover the top with more tips for added insulation.

rocks or a pole tied along its edge and hung behind the craft. Then pull the tarp forward and peg it down or weight it with rocks. The result is a crawl-in shelter.

Always build a shelter in cold country so the wind is broken from the interior. Also, whether in hot or cold country, never sleep directly on the ground (or snow) if you can possibly avoid it. Ground will be cold in the North, and in the desert when you are lying in shade in daytime it will be hotter at ground level than a bit above. Lay boughs or grass, anything available to make some space between your body and the ground.

Using trees. A second type of tarp shelter, in big-timber country, uses a large log, hopefully lying so it breaks the wind. The log must be at least a bit higher than your body will be when you lie down. The tarp or sheet is secured across the log and out from it, exactly as with a canoe, and a crawl-in shelter

A large log with a tarp secured on both sides gives protection from the wind.

Lean a pole into the crotch of a tree branch and drape the tarp over it, staking the edges; point the rear of the pole into the wind for a draft-proof shelter.

is thus available. Numerous other quick and easy shelters can be fashioned from tarp or sheet. Cut or break a pole. Lean it in a low tree crotch or against a low, stout branch, or lash it about three feet up against a tree trunk. Lay the tarp over this pole and weight or stake the edges. The rear end of the pole that touches or is thrust into the ground, should be pointed toward the wind, if cold, and the tarp brought clear to the ground on that end and weighted, to keep draft out.

A very common and easily made triangle tent of this kind is put over a pole frame. Cut one long pole and two shorter ones. The two short ones are the "shear poles." Thrust these into the ground with the butts at least as wide apart as the tent opening will be; lash the top ends together to form an X at the

Set up a triangle tent using two shear poles lashed together in an X at the top. Lay a long ridgepole into the X and slant it back to the ground. Spread the tarp across the ridgepole, and finish by weighting the outward edges.

top. The long ridgepole is laid into this X and slanted back to the ground. The tarp or sheet goes over the ridgepole and the tent is complete, staked or weighted at the outward slanted edges.

When you cut stakes simply cut forked sticks. Sharpen the upper (long) end and thrust it into the ground inverted so the fork holds the grommet. If you have difficulty with stakes, cut a fairly heavy pole for each side, lay these on the border on either side and tie the tarp to each. If you do cut stakes, and plan to abandon this shelter to keep traveling, take the stakes along. This saves time and effort the next afternoon.

A single pole lashed between two trees can be used to make two different types of simple shelters. Lashed

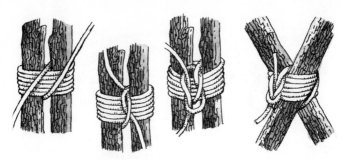

Strong lashings are essential to secure shelters. To join shear poles for erecting tents, lay two poles parrallel to each other. Make several turns around both poles, and one or two more turns of frapping between the poles and around the loops. Join the rope ends with a square knot and spread the poles apart to form the shears.

A lean-to made by lashing a pole between tree trunks and stretching the tarp to the ground leaves plenty of room for a fire out front if you need it.

at low height, the tarp is draped over it, drawn out at the bottom on each side and staked or weighted. This tent has two open ends. It is cool, keeps rain off. But if cold wind is a problem, the simple triangle shelter described above is better. The other type made with a pole lashed between two tree trunks is the simple lean-to. Lash the pole higher up, with one edge of the tarp secured to it, and the other edge pulled back on a slant and staked or weighted to the ground. A fire can be built in front of this lean-to, or in front of the other shelters, if one is needed.

Desert shelter. In a desert, a tarp can be laid atop several large sage bushes or other brush and tied for shade. In rocky places without trees or brush, stack up two rock piles spaced as wide as your tarp, each about two and one-half feet high. Lay a corner of the tarp atop each pile and weight it with another rock on top to hold it. Now draw the tarp back to its full length and make a lower pile of rocks for each

In the desert, a rock-and-tarp arrangement provides shade and slants downward for protection against rain.

rear corner. The corners are drawn atop these, and weighted to hold them down. Thus you have a shady shelter, slanted to keep off rain if need be. This type can be used in other than desert terrain, where rocks are the most abundant material. A pile along either side and at rear, banked with snow or dirt, also makes a fairly snug crawl-in shelter.

Building a lean-to. If your tarp is large enough, or you also have a sheet, or there are two or more peo-

> With a large tarp or plastic sheet, you can build a comfortable lean-to with closed ends. Attach the tarp to a pole lashed between two trees. Lash another pole to each tree, slanted the same way as the tarp, and pull the tarp ends around. Make sure the tent opening is out of the wind.

ple each with tarps, a large lean-to type shelter with closed ends can be made in numerous ways. One method uses the pole lashed between two trees. You secure tarps to it, then drape the ends over other poles lashed also to the trees and slanted out in the same direction as the tarp. This three-sided lean-to, with a good fire out front reflecting heat inside, is comfortable indeed. Wind direction should be either at an angle across or from behind. If you have a rope, you can eliminate the bother of cutting poles by using a rope for a ridgepole in any of these shelters.

Incidentally, many volumes showing primitive shelter go into detail about how to make a tepee. Shy away from this. Invariably, unless much work is involved, it will leak badly down the center, and it is difficult to keep a tarp or sheet in place. Stick with the very simple designs described thus far.

Natural Resources

Materials from forest and desert can be used to build and add to the comfort of these simple shelters. It may be that you are caught without so much as a tarp or sheet, perhaps with very little to use for lashings. You can still make suitable primitive shelters. Any lashings you can contrive from boot laces or pieces of cloth or string will be most helpful. Otherwise you will have to use twisted bark, tough grasses or reeds, or thin willow brush. Bear in mind that slabs of bark, often shown as material for roofing or siding a shelter, are extremely difficult to peel from large trees in any quantity. Unless time is no object, don't consider this.

Evergreen shelters. All across much of Canada, most of the northern U.S. and down the mountains of the U.S. and Mexico where emergencies are likely to occur, evergreen trees are abundant. The ones with the thickest branches, such as spruce, are best for shelter purposes, but any will do. The quickest, easiest shelter is made exactly as with the tarp, by cutting

In an area of evergreen trees, look for one with strong branches to which you can secure a pole. Lean smaller trees, ends jammed into the ground, on both sides of the pole for protection against wind and rain.

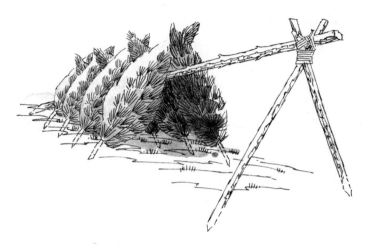

Leaning or lashing small evergreens to a ridge-pole supported by two shear poles allows space at the front for a fire.

a long pole, trimming off branches, and leaning it into a low crotch of a tree, or lashing it, leaned, to the trunk of a tree. If you are among evergreens, select a small, thick one, hopefully with branches coming close to ground. Lean the pole into its branches and secure it. The butt of the pole that touches the ground should point *toward* the wind if it is cold. Now cut small thick evergreens and lean or lash them against the pole from either side, their butts jammed into the ground. Lash tops if necessary. More evergreen branches cut and worked into the spreading limbs of the small evergreens will keep out more wind or rain.

Note that the thick spruce (if you used one) that holds the pole gives shelter from the front. If you want a fire out front, you cannot use this method, for the fire would be too close under the tree. In that case, you can cut three poles: one long one, two shorter ones, as described with tarp. If the earth is soft enough, sharpen the ends of the shorter ones, the shear poles, and thrust them into the ground so that the tops form a small X, and lash this point. Lean the long pole into the crotch thus formed, cut ever-

In dense areas of small spruce, lash together the tops of several small trees for a quick shelter. Clear a sleeping place and fill in spaces between trees with branches if necessary.

greens and lean or lash against each side of the long pole. Now you have a fair shelter and can have a fire by the opening.

If you find dense stands of small spruce, maybe six to eight feet tall, you can swiftly make a shelter by pulling the tops of several together and lashing them. First clear your sleeping place by cutting off inside branches. Then pull the tops down and tie them together, cutting more branches to weave easily into the sides and between the small trees, and you can get along. In dense stands of small evergreens of many varieties you can often make do without building a shelter. Simply find the thickest place you can and crawl in. Or where large evergreens have branches coming clear to the ground, cut off a very few and fashion a kind of den against the trunk. Much depends on weather.

One of the most interesting shelters I ever saw was thrown together by a guide in spruce country in northern Canada. He cut numerous small spruce boughs to make his bed and laid these near a big blowdown. Then he cut some spreading, large spruce boughs and set them over the blowdown. With this primitive frame as a base he began cutting more boughs and propping them, then laying small ones for a roof. In half an hour he had what can best be described as a "spruce-bough igloo" with a front opening away from prevailing wind. He slept in it for ten days while we hunted.

A pole cut and lashed, or laid in crotches, horizontally between two trees, with small evergreens

Another simple shelter is made by lashing a pole between trees and leaning small evergreens on both sides. Close up one end with more trees to keep out the wind.

leaned on either side, makes another type of shelter. Fill one end with other small evergreens to break the draft.

Treeless areas. Though most emergencies will arise where there is plentiful timber, some won't. In treeless or nearly treeless areas, numerous materials will suffice. Plentiful cattails make a fine shelter, like a duck blind. Invariably there is some bush, log, or tree which can hold them as a starter. Dense willows are another useful material. Tie the tops of a few bushes together and cut more to heap on and weave in. Willow or other brush plus cattails or heavy grass also forms a fine combination. Cut willows and thrust into high, dry ground as if you are making a duck blind. Weave cattails and other willows among these. Slant the ones that are thrust into the earth so the top opening is *narrow;* then you can cover it with more material. If it's too wide, your roof may fall in.

Sagebrush makes a good shelter, and in open country where it grows you may need one badly. Find the thickest, largest patch you can. This will be in a

Willow, cattails and heavy grass can be woven into good shelter. Stick branches into the ground on three sides, slanting them inward so the roof opening won't be too wide. Thread cattails and grass along the edges, and cover the roof.

depression or draw, which is all the better for it will be somewhat protected from wind. If there is a heavy stand of sage that can be left standing for a frame, use it. But cut a large amount to heap around. Any makeshift shelter erected from such materials, or even from rocks, will be best if made in a V or a "rounded V" shape. Support is better this way, and the roof can be more easily covered over.

> When you can't devise other shelter, try the protected area under the lip of a bank in a deep gully.

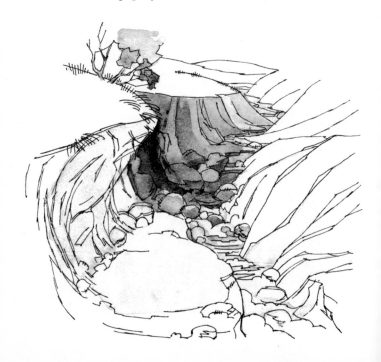

Mountains, even desert mountains or hills of the Southwest, have untold numbers of small caves or hollows beside a rock or under a ledge where you can find good shelter. In treeless rocky country, rock shelters can be constructed, but except for the man who will be staying there until rescued, they are not often worth the effort. Usually in this country there are deep, steep gullies that have eroded for centuries. Except in very rainy weather, you can usually find a protected place over the lip of such a bank. The deeper the erosion the better, as this means a flood would have to be of major proportions to fill it. Stay as close below the lip as possible. This measure is strictly for severe emergency, such as with a blizzard coming. Otherwise it is not a good idea to hole up in dry washes: in the desert sudden rains in nearby mountains might send flash floods pouring down. A cut bank may offer a good sleeping place, but watch the weather closely. Use an undercut wash bank in the desert for daytime shade only, and travel at night. Do your heavy sleeping in the forenoon. Keep in mind that summer storms are most likely to hit nearby mountains any time from noon on, but mornings will usually be clear.

Keep an eye out for caves, even small ones, or undercut rock ledges that are in the lee. Be wary of ledges that may not be stable or have precarious overhangs above. Watch out for snakes in caves. Large boulders may provide shelter, and evergreen boughs or other materials may be incorporated with them to good advantage. Don't fashion such a shelter too close to a streambank, however. In winter this might be safe. But in summer, especially in mountains, swift rises can occur, even though there is no rain where you are. It falls higher up the mountain and comes racing down.

Even if you have a sleeping bag you will be more comfortable by fixing up a mattress beneath it, and if you have no bag you will badly need some sort of bed. Evergreen boughs make an excellent one. So do heavy grasses, dry cattails, small willows, heaps of pine needles. Size up the immediate situation and see what is most plentiful. Boughs and marsh grass can be used as a covering if you have none.

An old comfort trick used by many explorers and pioneer trappers was to carry a "stuff bag." It was a piece of cloth sewn in the form of a simple sack. Today it can be made from tough nylon or any material that is very light yet will stand hard wear. Fold it as small as a handkerchief and carry it in a pocket or a pack. It can be used if need be for gathering berries, for carrying frogs while hunting them. It can serve when wet and inflated as a water-wing, or as a tote-bag for a dozen different chores on the trail. But its chief purpose among early wilderness travelers was as a pillow. Stuffed with grass or pine needles or even spruce twigs, it works very well and is simply emptied in the morning. Comfort in sleeping is important, and the little bag is a good item to have along.

Snow Shelters

You may be caught out in an area of deep snow. Shelters of brush and others so far described may be difficult to build. Instead of thinking of snow as your enemy, use it for the topnotch insulation it gives. Air temperature should guide your choice of shelters. For example, the lean-to is most valuable when the temperature is around zero or above. The snow cave, however, should not be built unless temperatures are relatively low, that is, below zero. This is because body heat will melt the roof when the thermometer reads between zero and twenty degrees.

Never set up shelter directly under a snow cornice

In the loosely drifted snow around a large tree, scoop out a hole around the trunk and crawl in under the branches for overnight shelter.

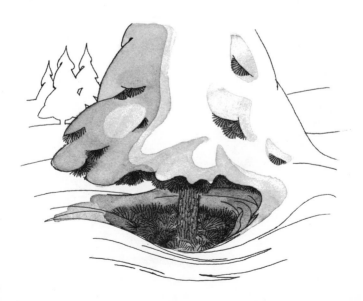

that might collapse. Look for and stay away from possible avalanche paths. Avoid locations where trees are all the same size at the edge of a steep draw. These are sure indicators of avalanche runs.

The kind of snow shelter you now build depends primarily upon the type of snow. If it is loosely

Hard snow several feet deep around a large tree provides warmer shelter. Dig down to the ground in a circle around the trunk, and use boughs for a bed at the bottom. Crawl in and curl up around the trunk for a comfortable sleep.

drifted, and you are in a forest, look for deep drifts around large trees. Crawl in under branches that are low hanging and scoop out a hole around the tree trunk. Use evergreen boughs for a bed and you will have a fairly snug den for overnight. Occasionally there will be a harder snow several feet in depth surrounding a large tree. In this case, dig down in a circle around the trunk, clear to the ground if possible. Cut boughs for the bottom for your bed, and you can curl up around the trunk. By laying other boughs for a roof, you will sleep warm and snug. If you have a candle, you can use it for a bit of warmth, or you can even build a small fire. But be sure to have ventilation through the boughs above.

One of the simplest snow shelters is a simple trench. This requires deep snow. You may find drifts deep enough and still in fairly protected places. Dig straight down, fashioning a trench long enough to lie in. The snow must be firm enough for the sides to hold. The roof, if you have tarp or sheet, is covered, and rocks, sticks, or blocks of snow weight its edges. Or you can cover the top with evergreen branches, or with poles into which grass or brush is woven. If the snow is firm, poles laid across the top with chunks of snow atop them furnish cover. In any snow shelter, however, be sure to select a location where you won't get drifted in without any ventilation. Leave an opening or keep a stick thrust up through your roof or along its edge so you can make sure there is an opening beside it.

If you find a large snow drift that is fairly firm, dig a hole into the side of the drift. Dig *toward* the wind, to keep the entrance both out of the wind and

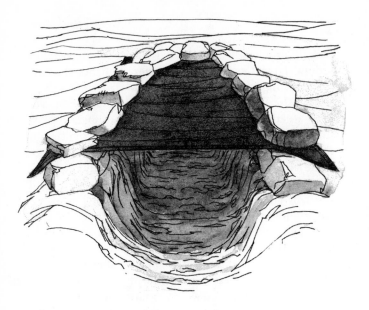

To make a snow trench, dig out an area long enough to lie in. Stretch a tarp across the top for a roof, and weight the edges with rocks or snow blocks.

from drifting full. If the drift is not large enough to make a hole allowing you to get clear back inside, at least you will have a good windbreak and insulation behind you. Place boughs or whatever you can scrounge inside for a bed. And, if possible make a pole crisscross base outside and build a small fire on it. Snow inside will not melt and you can get some warmth. If the drift doesn't have a firm crust, about two to three feet thick, and you are afraid the roof will collapse, two solutions are possible. Gather boughs

You can build a windbreak shelter by digging a hole into the side of a large, firm drift, making room for a bough bed and a fire. Keep the entrance out of the wind.

if available, and arch strong feathered ones inside. Or, remove the snow roof entirely, cover thickly with boughs and then replace snow. If you have no fire inside any snow shelter, you will have ample ventilation with all the holes well plugged. The smaller the space for you, the better your snow insulation will work. Try to avoid working so hard you perspire heavily while making the shelter, or you will chill badly later.

If you happen to find a very large drift formation where there is no avalanche danger from above but where the drift is on a slope, it may be possible to start rather low down, digging up on a slant to form an entrance tunnel. Then round out a sleeping cave in the snow above, as on a ledge. You can form a snow

Under ideal conditions, build a snow cave by digging an entrance tunnel leading to a sleeping area. Use a snow block for the entrance "door" and a stick thrust through the top of the cave for ventilation.

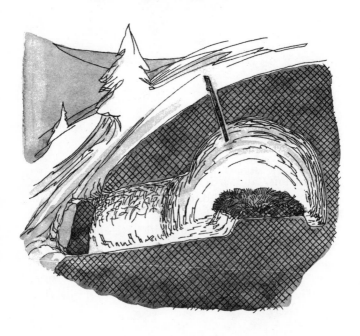

block to partially plug the entrance. A stick carried inside and thrust from your cave through to the outside on the slant of the drift will give a ventilation hole, and it can be kept clear by a thrust of the stick when necessary. This is a rather elaborate snow shelter. It requires *well-crusted snow*. Don't plan on being lucky enough very often to find this ideal combination of drift and packed snow.

Eskimos have made igloos of snow blocks since ancient times. This is a long, difficult process and requires far too much time and energy for the emergency situation. However, *if* the snow is hard packed and crusty, and *if* there is enough of it, you may be able to cut out blocks to form a shelter. Blocks stacked for a windbreak in a U shape or V shape will be better than nothing. It may be possible to dig a trench, then cut blocks to lay across it, on supporting poles. Rectangular blocks might be propped in inverted V shape, one leaned from either side to touch the other, forming the V apex above the trench.

While such methods are valuable to know, don't plan on being able to utilize them. Cutting blocks of hard-packed snow is not easy, and it is not likely that you will have tools to accomplish it. At a stalled vehicle or downed plane you may. Otherwise, probably your only tools will be a belt axe (which will do the job) or a knife (which may not do it without massive expenditure of energy). In any emergency, always measure possible results against the amount of work involved. Save and conserve strength at all times. Ponder the problem: is there an easier way?

A variation on the igloo calls for a trench covered by rectangular blocks propped against each other in an inverted V shape.

All of the foregoing should emphasize the good sense of having a tarp or sheet along so shelter is that much simpler to fashion. As you travel on any expedition, always watch for possible bivouacs. Remember to learn to observe. Here are two big boulders close together beside a river. A few branches staked between them equals shelter. There is a big upturned tree with roots spreading. Tie the tarp to them, or lop some branches and build a shelter with the roots as a base. There is an enormous log on the ground. The tarp, or a few branches, can make a primitive crawl-in within minutes.

I would suggest, too, that you occasionally make an overnight adventure out of actually *building* a primitive shelter and staying in it. On a deer hunt, let's say, come into camp some afternoon and make a nearby shelter for yourself out of whatever is at hand. Stay in it for a night or two. Reading instructions is fine, but there is nothing like the real experience!

11 / Signaling for Help

IN AN EARLIER CHAPTER ("What You Need For Emergencies"), signaling devices were briefly mentioned. It is imperative that you know how to attract help, or make your presence known. Once again, if you have filed a trip plan with someone and do not return on schedule, a search for you will undoubtedly be underway. In that event the searchers will have at least a rough idea of where to do their searching. But if you did not leave word where you were going, or deviated from your plan—both serious omissions—then searchers must work rather haphazardly. To assist them, you must do a good job of making your whereabouts known, at times making it possible for searchers to know where you have been.

Signals for help are aimed at two human senses: sight and hearing. Searchers using aircraft are for all practical purposes restricted to picking up sight signals. Ground searchers may be able to pick up both sight and sound. The chance of sound signals being heard is only fair, however, for sounds you can make travel over only very limited distances. In addition, searchers on the ground, especially in hilly or mountainous and timbered terrain, may have difficulty pinpointing exact direction of sounds. Results are amazing, for example, when you are out hunting in mountains with several companions. Ask each member of the party, when a shot is heard, precisely where he thinks it originated. Especially with whimsical breezes in rough terrain, there may be as many opinions as there are people.

Sound Signals

Nonetheless, if you possess a firearm, and ammunition, shot signals may be helpful. However, do not be eager to fire your gun. It is useless to fire away indiscriminately, when there is no good reason to believe anyone may hear. Save the ammo. Much will depend on where you are. If you know without question that you are in an area where other hunters are certain to be, then a series of three evenly spaced shots may bring someone to your aid. It is a good plan to save your shots until you are sure that any hunters within hearing—camped, for example, or leaving the forest for the day—will be most *likely* to hear.

Just at full dark, when it is too dark to shoot game, is one of the best times.

Other hunters may not realize you have an emergency and will not be aware that your shots are asking for help. However, after dark, three evenly spaced shots may get attention. If you know searchers are out, shots may be helpful. But under today's somewhat crowded hunting conditions, and unfortunately with all too many hunters firing away indiscriminately and missing too much, shots may not be very efficient signals. In a true wilderness breakdown or crash, or when you are lost far from any outpost of civilization, it is best to horde ammunition against your need to use it in gathering food. Whatever you do, don't waste those last two or three cartridges on a wild attempt to make a hearable sound.

There could be an exception. If you actually heard searchers near you, but they missed you, then shooting is a legitimate endeavor. Or, if you hear a chain saw, let's say, or a snowmobile, or any human sound distantly, whether it is dark or daylight, wait until there is a lull in the sound (the saw stops momentarily, for example) and then fire your three evenly spaced shots.

Shouting is usually a total waste. It requires much energy. It can injure your throat if you keep at it. Worst of all, the sound of your own shouts may produce panic. If you know searchers are trying to find you and *you hear them* but you are in dense brush or perhaps injured, then by all means shout. Cup your hands and shout in the direction of the sound. If possible go toward the sound and shout. This applies if sounds you hear are not from searchers but, say, from a survey or forestry party, a group of hunters —anyone passing through.

If you have a defunct means of transport, hammering on metal with tools can send a sound message to searchers or someone passing within hearing. This sound carries much farther than a shout and because it is an *unusual* sound in the wilderness, it may draw attention that shots would not. Further, it does not require undue expenditure of energy.

The best sound signal is a whistle. Signal whistles that blow loud and are high-pitched are available in good sports stores. One packed in your gear, as suggested, could save your life. Blowing a whistle takes much less energy than shouting, and it can be heard much farther. It is also an unexpected sound in the wilderness. To someone not on a search mission, and to someone who is searching, it is a sound to home in on. Whistle from a ridge top, or out in the open, to give the sound waves the best chance to travel. I repeat, use it when you feel there is the best chance for someone to hear.

You must also keep yourself alert for *hearing* sounds. This applies to sighting a plane too. Stay as much as possible where you will be able to hear (and see) help. A snow shelter in which you may have to hole up is insulated from sound. If there are others with you, take turns standing watch, and listening.

It is even possible that by whistling to imitate the dots and dashes of the Morse Code, you can form an SOS message. Conceivably a listener would not know the Code. Nonetheless, evenly spaced "dots and

When ground signals are seen by an airplane, there is a standard response. If your message was received and understood, the plane will rock from side to side; at night, it will flash green lights in the signal lamps. If your message was received and not understood, the plane will make a complete circle; at night, it will flash red signals.

dashes" of whistling may catch attention because of the peculiarity of the sound pattern.

Sight Signals

Numerous sight signals can be utilized. Here we should go back to a type of sight signal more commonly associated with travel in the wilderness (see Chapter 6). I am speaking about marking a trail. The traditional method in forest country is by blazes. Suppose you have decided to leave a stranded means of transport and strike out. By blazing your trail well (assuming you have a hatchet or knife) you make it easier for someone searching for you, who comes upon the vehicle, to know where you went. Or, if you are lost, and even if you are not but must walk out, someone may cut your freshly blazed trail and catch up with you. Especially if you are lost, blazes will lead a searcher to you.

When you are initially in an emergency, if you make forays out and back as I suggested earlier, blazes can be used advantageously. You should have at least a basic idea of what they mean. Experienced oldtime woodsmen made small blazes. You should make large ones. The ordinary blaze is a spot where you have hacked a slab of bark off a tree. A single blaze, centered on the trunk in your travel direction, marks your trail. In the traditional system, this single blaze also means that you are going *away from your camp*. Now that blaze won't do you any good coming back. So, you must blaze the other side of the tree, too, making certain that you can see any blaze for some distance ahead of or behind you. On the far side of

> Familiarize yourself with the basic trail blazes. A single blaze in the center of a tree indicates your travel directions away from camp. A small blaze to the right or left of the center blaze indicates a right or left turn. When it is not possible to use trees, mark your trail with rocks pointing straight ahead or to the left or right, or use logs arranged like an arrow in your travel direction. Remember to mark the far side of a blazed tree so you can read your way back.

the tree you place two blazes, one directly above the other. This marks your trail *back to camp*.

Blazes give a follower confidence that he is going in the right direction on your trail. He'll either catch up, or meet you. When you make a turn, make your regular "going away" blaze; then below and to the side of the trunk in the direction of your turn (right or left) make another blaze. When you do this, make a "going away" blaze in the new direction on a nearby tree, so that no one can miss exactly where you are headed.

Perhaps there will be no trees large enough to blaze. There are other types of trail markings, many of them used long ago by Indians and known to seasoned outdoorsmen. For example, if there is brush, break or cut sections and in plainly visible places lay them so the cut butt points in the trail direction. If you make a right or left turn, lay one that way, then break another nearby to emphasize direction. Rocks can be used, too. Small, easily visible piles mark the trail. A pile with a single rock on the right side means you turned that way, and vice versa. But make another cairn right away, again to be emphatic. Knotted marsh grass can mark a trail, and you can even indicate where you rafted across a lake or started rafting down a stream by sharpening stakes and thrusting them into earth of shore or bank, leaning in the direction of travel. When rafting a stream, pause if possible quite regularly to leave some kind of easily visible marker.

Incidentally, if you leave others, injured or otherwise, at the scene of a debacle and you start to walk out, bear on your person a written message, contrived even with charcoal if necessary, telling the situation and location of the others. If you are alone, and you can keep a brief diary as you go, do so. It will help someone who rescues you in the event you are hurt or weak, to know when and what you ate, etc.

Flares, Candles, and Dyes

Hopefully you will have tucked away in your pack, as suggested, some signal flares and smoke candles. There are several types of flares. The large ones are thrust into the ground and ignited. Planes and vehicles, should have a supply of these. The other type, very small and compact, that can be squirreled away and carried while walking is for shooting into the air. There is a small "gun" and several small flares in the typical package. These are available in sporting goods stores, and if not a store manager can help you get them. The gun is a small tube-like gadget to be held in the hand. You fire the flare from it and the experience is about like shooting a small-caliber pistol. The flare streaks upward. You should shoot it straight up, always in the open if at all possible, and from a ridge if in hilly country. It may reach 75 to 150 feet, leaving a fiery red trail behind and a burst of red flame at the top. There is also a "bang" as the burst appears at the top of the flight. Flares can be useful in guiding both ground searchers and aircraft to you. But be advised not to shoot flares in hope. Don't waste this precious signal until you *know it can be seen.* An aircraft passing over can see it.

Ground searchers can see it. But know that they are there before you fire. Otherwise you simply waste a very precious signal.

The same applies to the commercial smoke signals. Both flares and smoke candles that emit yellow smoke, available from the same outlets, are brief signals. Each lasts only 30 seconds or so. It is foolish to waste these items unless you are trying desperately to guide a known and sighted (or heard) searcher to you. It is a good idea to carry several of these smoke candles.

Especially nowadays the primary search mission is handled by aircraft. Thus much emergency signaling is tied to aircraft in some way. Signals visible by aircraft are very common nowadays, whereas in past years they were not. Dyes to make a splash of color on water or on snow are common as standard equipment in aircraft flying into wilderness areas. Water dyes should not be used until actually needed, for they may be swept away. Dyes used on snow in severe cold, orange or other colors, will stay put. These might be available if you are in a wilderness plane emergency and the plane is not demolished. But be sure to use such dyes downwind and not over food. Don't get them onto yourself either.

Signal Fires

Such modern methods of signaling are not always available, however. More likely you will have to build a signal fire, or mark out a message in snow, sand, or by piles of rocks. Many searchers, and others, may not know that *two* signal fires sending up smoke quite close together were the original signal that someone was lost. Today a series of *three*—sounds, light flashes, fires—is more generally recognized as a plea. Perhaps you won't be able to handle that many fires. In a total wilderness, smoke even from one fire will certainly draw attention—from anyone who is watching. In National Forests and State Forests, fire towers and patrol planes watch for smoke, even in the Primitive and Wilderness Areas. They must. Chances that smoke will be seen are good. Don't try to start a forest fire. This is a bit ridiculous. You can get caught in it, or destroy thousands of acres of forest when you don't need to.

Regardless of your situation—downed plane, stalled vehicle, lost—build your big bonfire in the *open* where it cannot start a real conflagration. The bright fire itself will be useful at night. Smoke is more useful by day. Gather your material carefully. Lay the big fire, but have green boughs or grass or green brush ready. When the blaze gets going in fine shape, smother the fire temporarily with the green material. This sends up a billow of white smoke. Oil from a plane engine also creates smoke. So will tires; this will be black smoke.

Use judgment about when to start a fire. If you are lost, there is no harm in trying to attract someone's attention with a high-rising smoke. The weather will have great bearing on your success. If you are staying in one place, waiting for rescue, the best idea is to have the fires laid and ready—even to coals always going if possible—to touch off the big blaze when a plane shows up distantly. In spruce country you could even set fire to a big lone tree out in the open. You have to prime it first by laying grass and brush in lower branches to get it started.

If fuel is easily gathered, and you are staying put, certainly there is no harm in keeping a signal fire going constantly. The more remote your position, the more attention it is certain to draw from anyone in the region. A big smoke in any National Forest, where a high percentage of lost persons and other emergencies occur, you can bet will eventually be seen and checked by some distant tower man. But it is inexcusable to take chances on destroying thousands of acres when you will undoubtedly be rescued without that. Be sure a fire is out in the open—on a ridge, a beach, a sandbar, a wide meadow—where it or its smoke can be readily seen from the ground or the air. Keep in mind, too, that a bright *blaze* in the open at night, as atop a ridge at timberline as an example, may well be more effective than attempts at smoke signals. Illustrations in books too often show that lovely smoke towering straight up for several hundred feet—but in reality it seldom does. Often the smoke hugs the ground or is dissipated by weather.

Fire and smoke are likely to be most useful and easiest to use in the amount needed when an emergency concerns a stalled vehicle or a downed plane. That is, when oil and gas are available. Consider making some sort of container, even a hole dug into sand or clay, and then igniting oil or gasoline poured over it. The earth holds the flammable liquid but causes it to burn steadily. Stand back when igniting! If no gas or oil is available you must depend on green

SURVIVORS USE LIFERAFT
SAILS TO CONVEY SIGNALS

YELLOW

BLUE

ON LAND: Should we wait for rescue plane? AT SEA: Notify rescue agency of my position

ON LAND AND AT SEA: Plane is flyable, need tools

ON LAND AND AT SEA: Need first aid and supplies

AT SEA: Need equipment as indicated. Signals follow

ON LAND: Need gas and oil, plane is flyable

ON LAND AND AT SEA: Need medical attention

ON LAND AND AT SEA: Need food and water

LAND AND SEA: Do not attempt landing

ON LAND: Walking in this direction AT SEA: Drifting Have abandoned plane

ON LAND: Need warm clothing AT SEA: Need exposure suit

ON LAND AND AT SEA: Arrow shows landing direction OK to land

ON LAND: Civilization Indicate direction AT SEA: Rescue craft

ON LAND: Need quinine or atabrine AT SEA: Need sun cover

or damp *fine* fuels—grass, cattails, feathery evergreen branches—to be laid on a good blaze to make smoke.

There is hardly a place left on this continent today where someone won't soon sight smoke, fire, or other sign that a human is in distress. In some ways this is sad, but not to the person waiting to be rescued. Another point of encouragement is that each year a few magazines print the stories of persons who got into awesome difficulty and barely got out, or sometimes didn't make it. However, the reason these stories reach print is that the incidents are so *rare*. So, be confident. Today there is almost "no place to hide."

A vehicle with a CB radio in it, or a downed plane with a radio that still works, is the best survival aid in a poor situation. Be wary of running down a battery, unless a motor can be started to charge it. Almost always someone will be listening and will pick up even the most garbled message, if the distance is not too great. A "fix" on *where* is far more important than what you may have to say. Keep it in mind. Don't pour out your anguished tale. Try to get across the message of *where*.

The Signal Mirror

Of all signaling devices known in our air-rescue age, possibly the most useful one is the smallest, simplest one, the one least used, and carried, by the average outdoorsman. Everyone, as it is said, talks about it, or knows about it, but nobody happens to have one. This is the signaling mirror. You should have one in your pack! This is not just an ordinary mirror. It

is of the type used by the armed services and you can usually buy it in surplus stores or marine supply stores. The ordinary mirror can be made to work, and you should try it if that is all you have. But sighting it properly so the flash can be seen by a plane is difficult. The signal mirror is easily and accurately sighted.

It has a hole in it. This is the sighting hole. You must keep the mirror polished brightly. Sight through the hole, holding the mirror just a few inches from your face. If you are looking in a direction that is

The first step in using a signal mirror is to sight through the hole, holding the mirror a few inches from your face, at the cockpit of the aircraft. Next, look in the mirror reflection for the spot of sunlight shining on your face through the hole. Adjust the mirror until the spot of light coincides with the hole, and you will be flashing signals directly to the plane.

If the sun and the aircraft form an obtuse angle, pick up the spot of light from the sun on your hand. Hold the mirror as before, and sight the plane through the hole. Then tilt the mirror until the spot appears on your hand. Find the spot in the mirror reflection, and line it up with the hole to flash signals. It is easier to catch the spot on your hand if you hold the mirror on the side of the sun and stretch out your other hand below it.

partially toward the sun, so that aircraft and sun are both within your view and the two of them within no more than a 90 degree arc, a spot of bright light will fall upon your face, through the hole. Note that this spot is reflected also in the rear side of the mirror, which also has a polished surface. Sight through the hole at the aircraft, or from an open ridge toward any possible rescue source, and change the angle of the mirror, while keeping sighted, until the spot of light is no longer seen. This means that it is now in perfect alignment with the sighting hole, and that flashes will be seen by the plane or distant observer.

This won't work if the sun and rescue source form, with you at the ground-based apex, an obtuse angle. This would mean the angle between sun and the

point to which you wish to direct the flashes is *more* than 90 degrees. Now hold the mirror, again only a few inches from your face, and sight through the hole at the aircraft. But, you must now tilt the mirror more, to pick up reflection from the sun. You can do this most easily by holding the mirror in the hand on the side where the sun is, and holding your other palm flat and outstretched below it, to pick up the spot of light. It can't strike your face now for it will be angled too low, but it will strike upon your hand. Now, continuing to sight on the plane, adjust the mirror again until the spot disappears, that is, coincides with the hole. This operation is much harder and it is a good idea to *practice* from varied angles with a signal mirror so you know how to succeed with it.

Few persons realize how far mirror flashes will carry. For best results the air should be clear and the sun bright, of course, but surprisingly strong reflections are given on hazy days and at least weak ones on modestly overcast days. If you are really "socked in" the mirror isn't usable. It is easiest to send mirror signals into the air. A pilot at a great distance can pick them up. Thus, if you hear but cannot see an aircraft, make diligent horizon sweeps with the mirror in that direction. The flashes can be seen even when you cannot see the plane. Even when you neither see nor hear any aircraft, using the mirror in long sweeps of the horizon can do no harm and just may offer a pickup signal to someone. On a seacoast or shore of a large lake, use a mirror to signal to ships. If you are not lost, but in some difficulty, study your

map and look for locations of fire towers, Forest
Service lookouts. You may discover that one is within
several miles, so you can take a compass fix on it and
aim your mirror signal in that direction. It is a good
idea to persevere with such signaling. Keep at it!
Don't give up.

Let's presume, however, that you have no mirror.
Search your gear, or vehicle or downed plane, for a
substitute. The easiest way to make one is from the
lid of or a piece of a tin can. Punch a hole through
the center of it. If you have nothing to make a round
hole, punch it through with a knife blade in an X,
and ream it out a bit with a small stick. Don't get
it too large. Polish the lid as shiny as you can, selecting the side that shines brightest for signaling. Now

> If you don't have a signal mirror, a homemade
> one from the lid of a tin can works the same
> way. Punch a hole, not too large, through the
> center. Polish the lid as well as possible, and
> use the shinier side to face the plane.

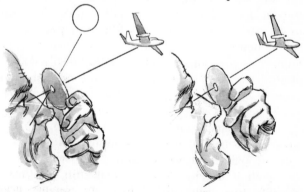

use this exactly as we have described for the signal mirror.

Lights make good signals—a flashlight, a lantern, a torch. The trouble is you are not likely to have these. Also, a flashlight beam even in full dark is not seen as far or as emphatically as the flash of a signal mirror on a bright day. Nonetheless, use lights if they are available and if the situation seems appropriate. You can flash a pine torch by holding it in the open, then obscuring it behind a branch or your jacket hung over a branch. Try such signals, with any light available, at night. But if an active search is on for you and aircraft are aloft, a big signal fire will be more valuable.

Morse Code

This is a good place, to mention Morse Code. There are divergent opinions on whether you should memorize the Code for the entire alphabet. It is not a bad idea to have this Code and some other signals to be mentioned in a moment folded in a small waterproof packet in your duffle. Whatever your emergency, however, in signaling for help what you are doing is sending an SOS. This is so universally known as a call for "HELP" that probably you need no more Morse Code than enough to form the letters S-O-S. An S is three dots. An O is three dashes. Thus, ... --- ... spells out SOS, which anyone at all familiar with the Code will know means you need help. You can spell it out with a light, with a whistle. You can spell it out by waving a makeshift flag, made possibly from your shirt. There are waving (flag)

movements that are universally standard for the Code. The S-O-S signal is made by waving three times on the right, three on the left, three on the right. It is up to you whether or not to try to learn all of the Code. My theory is that the signal described is known to almost everyone, but the complete Code and its corresponding flag movements seldom are. Keep it simple for all concerned.

Ground Letters

In any type of terrain you can probably contrive to spell out in huge letters on the ground or snow

A pile of brush in the form of a huge letter can be seen by an airplane or other distant observer.

the fact that you need help. Keep this simple, too.
You can form a single word or sign: SOS, HELP, or
LOST. In an open place on a steep, high mountain
this would be visible from the valley below. But most
such signals will be directed at the chance of sighting
from an aircraft. Bear in mind that the effectiveness
of your sign depends almost entirely upon how much
contrast you can arrange.

> Tramp out letters in the snow as deep as pos-
> sible, and slant them so the sun casts shadows
> across for contrast.

For example, all tracks (such as animal tracks) show best when the light hits at an angle across them. This is because the side of a track then casts a shadow. Thus, if snow is deep, tromp out the letters S-O-S, or one of the other words, as deep as possible and so slanted that both morning and afternoon sun will cast shadows *across* your sign. This gives you the best chance of a sign plainly seen from above. However, if there are evergreens around, tromp out your signal, then cut branches and stuff into the letters. This makes a very dark sign upon a light background. Other dark material can be used: willow brush darker than the snow, etc.

In sand or soft earth you may have to depend entirely on shadows for contrast. At a seashore or on a broad, dry sandbar, pour water into the letters to make them darker than dry sand. If you are in rocky country, dark rocks will spell out your message on light ground. If rocks are close to the earth color, pile them up to spell a word and again depend on shadows for contrast.

In dense brush or a swamp, you have a problem in forming such a signal. But be ingenious. If you are staying at the spot, try to clear brush entirely from an area. This will make a spot to catch attention from above. Turn over sod to make letters. Cut brush to form them. Any strips of cloth can be laid out to form a signal. In fact, if you know a search is on, scatter anything of contrast that you can find. Drape rags on bushes. Climb a tree and tie a cloth that will wave in the wind. Try *anything* that may draw attention from an aircraft. Suppose you are in the North

and beside a lake that is frozen over. *You* may be difficult to sight. But dark spruce limbs, any dark gear or heaps of logs laid out on the ice will show up handsomely. Spell your appeal here.

Remember that a downed plane or stalled vehicle may not be in a spot where it is easily seen. It is in fact amazing how downed planes can virtually disappear right in well-settled country. You cannot predict where the crippled transport will be. However, make every attempt to clean off upper surfaces so that they will shine or show to best advantage. Keep wiping snow off. Shine any surface that will reflect. Occasionally you can haul sections of a smashed machine out where light will be reflected from them. Again, always think in terms of *contrast*.

Ground-To-Air Signals

Contrast is important if you use some of the signals that have come to be standard for ground to air display. Almost all airmen will know these. They are of three types, and you will find illustrations here to show the principles involved. One is the Emergency Code, Ground-to-Air that has come into wide use in search and rescue missions. These are simple *symbols,* to be formed in snow or with rocks or brush exactly as described for the SOS. Each symbol has its special meaning. Actually it is not necessary for you to know

Make the symbols of the ground-to-air emergency code shown at right from any material you have, including rocks, snow or brush.

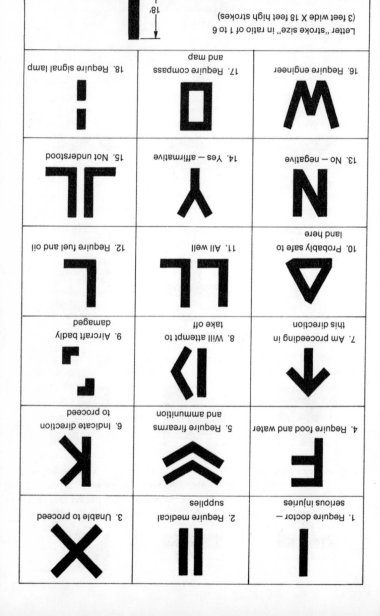

all of these. If you do carry a packet, waterproofed, with such material in it (as the Morse Code) the entire list is handy to have. But if you do not know all or have all, by all means know a few important ones. For example, one single long stroke, like a plain Figure 1, means there is serious injury and that a doctor is required. Two such strokes side by side indicate the need for medical supplies. A big X means you are unable to proceed, that is, move from where you are. A large arrow design means you are going to travel in the direction you have made it point. It could even indicate you *have* left in that direction. A large plain K is a question, asking that the aircraft indicate which way you should travel. It is possible an aircraft cannot land but can guide you out. A large F is a request for both food and water. These are the symbols you will need most, but as noted it is a valid idea to know all of them, or have them with you.

The second type of signal system is a series of designs formed by cloth panels. These are termed the Ground, Sea and Air Visual Code, Panel Emergency Signals. They were designed for armed services use, for survivors. The panels are in blue and yellow. It is obvious that most persons in the type of emergencies about which we are talking will not be equipped

The panel signals for the ground, sea and air emergency visual code shown at left can be made by a standard panel with contrasting colors on either side. If you don't have a panel, use a blanket, and cloth, earth, snow, or anything at hand to show contrast.

with such signal panels. However, without any doubt a searching pilot who saw the panel signals simply in black and white, or contrasting intermediate shades, made with earth, snow, rocks, brush or cloth if at hand, would immediately recognize them. Again, only three or four are of significance to the type of wilderness emergency we are thinking about. But the Panel Code is illustrated here nonetheless.

A code more likely to be useful is made up of *body signals*. This is termed the International Ground-Air Body Signal Code and is well known to pilots generally. Here also you would not ordinarily need to know all of the signals, but you certainly should know those of greatest importance in emergencies. Lying flat on your back with arms extended above your head indicates that medical assistance is urgently needed. This is *not* to be used indiscriminately, as for a slightly ill person. It means a matter of life and death. If an aircraft attempts to pick you up but you know it is not safe to land, stand erect and with arms extended upward wave both back and forth at same time, in same direction, across your face. If it is safe to land, squat on your heels, face landing direction, extend arms straight out in front of chest, pointing same direction as your body. If you have abandoned a vehicle or downed plane, or even a campsite, you indicate that you need urgently to be picked up by standing erect and holding both arms extended upward. There are others, as shown. These are of most importance.

Knowledge of all the signaling techniques discussed here will be of unlimited value to you in emergencies.

Body signals are internationally known and easy to do.

But it is far better to dodge the emergency than to have to use the signals! You cannot predict where a plane may go down. But it is a fact that most of the vehicle breakdowns or bog-downs could have been avoided by caution. Getting lost, or caught without the necessaries, is invariably the result of carelessness either in preparation or on the trail!

12 / Weather

No TRIP-A-YEAR outdoorsman can hope to be a super-expert weather forecaster. But anyone who intends to spend a lot of time in the outdoors should store up knowledge about the weather fundamentals that apply anywhere. In addition it is wise to know in detail the weather signs and patterns of the region you visit the most.

Let me illustrate briefly. In my region of Texas I can expect the period from about mid-June to September to be extremely dry. During that time if we do get a rain, it just might be a real gully-washer. In the April-May period in normal years there will be rains, sometimes heavy ones. After the dry summer, September launches rains again. But from mid-October through to about Christmas we will probably have pretty fair weather and although late afternoons may get cloudy, there will usually be a bright hour before sundown. That knowledge is important to me in planning dates when I need to shoot a lot of still or movie film.

Around Christmas and through early February we get our cold weather; every year nobody believes it will be as cold as it really gets. Then we'll have a sudden respite, with too-hot weather for a few days. This is the very general pattern. But I like to know, and must know for photo purposes, such things as when the leaves come out again, as well as when they fall. Grouse hunters and deer hunters should know, too. Trips can be planned ahead with such knowledge.

Weather and Survival

When it comes to emergencies and survival situations, a knowledge of what "it" is going to do after you're in trouble can be most valuable. You need to know the general patterns for an area: When is freeze-up generally due? Is a big snowstorm in mid-October likely to herald full winter, or is it just a first one that will be followed by a clear and thawing period? From which direction are the prevailing winds here? You must know what various weather *signs* mean to the *immediate* future. Long range forecasting isn't as important and can't be too accurately doped anyway.

I'd like to give you two examples. First, a general pattern valuable to know. In the high country of the western mountains during summer, it is common for day after day to dawn beautifully clear, crisp and cloudless. If you are not filled in on high-country summers, you might start off on a hike with no jacket, no rain-jacket, or no poncho tied behind the saddle. But the mountain-wise outdoorsman knows that he had better get his fishing or hiking or riding or picture-taking done before noon, or two p.m. at the latest.

By mid-morning fluffy white (cumulus) clouds will begin to appear. Between noon and two as a rule little showers hit the high slopes. Some of the white clouds become dark. By late afternoon the real deluges let go in spots. You may or may not quit by dusk, when there is usually a short period of sunshine, often followed by drizzle during the night. Yet the morning is almost certain to be clear again. Mountain tops, as it's said in the West, are "where weather comes from."

Relate this to an emergency situation. The well-informed person knows this pattern is almost certain to occur. He starts traveling very early, and if the weather picture begins to build as described, he gets into shelter or begins to fix shelter and get his cooking done during midday or early afternoon. What might fool you is that some of the sky may still be lovely blue, with big cumulus clouds drifting. In fact, only small showers may occur. But up a canyon a black cloud might be moving down toward where you are. They come along swiftly in the mountains and severe storms are often upon you before there's time to get a rain suit out.

Now for a second, more specific example. You are anywhere on the east slope of the Rockies, not necessarily in the mountains. You could be way down in west Texas or eastern Wyoming. It is fall. The day is almost balmy, with a small breeze from the southwest. But presently you notice the breeze is switching directions, to the west and then around to the northwest, and there are a few little clouds that old hands sometimes call "mare's tails"—little whitish skeins—in the west and northwest. They multiply. The northwestern horizon soon loses its blue. The wind rises steadily and now is definitely from the northwest and north. All these signs are yelling at you to get under cover. This could be a fake, but in fall nine times out of ten it signals a howling blizzard within a few hours. It may pass quickly, that is, after one severe day.

The weather on this east slope all the way down to the Texas and Mexico Gulf Coast originates in the Northwest and sweeps southeast. Fronts in fall are numerous and commonly move fast—furiously, too. I have seen the temperature on a still, sultry, overcast fall day drop 50 degrees in a few hours with a whistling norther in progress. This could be serious for you. But knowing the signs gives you time to make your shelter and secure it well against the blow, and probably the snow.

On either seacoast weather patterns may differ from those within the entire interior of the U.S. and Canada, because of proximity to the oceans. Most emergencies will occur in the interior simply because it

is so much larger, has more outdoorsmen moving in
it, and contains the major share of wilderness. If you
could carry a barometer, you would have good odds
on weather-forecasting anywhere. But this isn't possible. So, most of the signs you should know concern
wind and clouds.

Clouds

My feeling is that wind direction is a more accurate
indicator than clouds, for the simple reason that many
cloud formations are complex and confusing. But although one type blends into another as weather
changes, and a lost or stranded person has enough to
do to keep himself together without trying to dope
out the intricacies, some cloud knowledge is certainly
necessary.

We've already mentioned the big, fluffy white
cumulus clouds. In most regions they are common in
warm-to-hot weather. They build from none or few
in morning to many towering ones in the afternoon,
and may bring high-altitude storms from noon on. At
lower altitudes they usually bring thundershowers, or
at least portend them, by late p.m. to night. A darken-
ing section of sky, in any direction, among such
clouds indicates spotty or widespread storms.

If there are *nimbus* clouds, you'll know it. They
are very low and without special form, in large dark
masses or overcasts. Ordinarily when they are present
it is already raining or snowing or will shortly. *Cirrus*
clouds are wispy and white, bits of fair-weather clouds
blown to feathery designs by high-altitude breezes. But

Basic cloud formations. Wispy, high-altitude cirrus clouds mean fair weather. Fluffy, white cumulus clouds may bring high-altitude storms in the afternoon, or evening thundershowers in lower altitudes. Lower, dark and stormy nimbus clouds appear in rainy or snowy weather. Long, low-altitude stratus clouds mean that rain or snow conditions are not far off.

watch these closely. They are the so-called "mare's tails," and if their numbers grow you can be pretty sure that within a few hours to a day something is going to happen, rain or snow. *Stratus* clouds look like the name sounds, long, low banks of clouds. These may not immediately bring rain or snow, but they indicate that such conditions are "making up."

Again, cloud formations are constantly changing, so that combinations such as stratocumulus, cirrostratus, etc., appear. A study of these evolutions can be puzzling. I believe a knowledge of the four basic cloud formations is enough. Otherwise, in an already difficult situation you can become more confused. *Wind direction,* plus the four cloud types, gives you about all the clues you need.

Wind

Of course, what the barometer is doing is important: rising, falling, doing either swiftly, or slowly, or holding steady. You can't guess too accurately about that, although if you study a barometric pattern at home you will know by sky and wind "feel" what it is doing. If you know the direction from which the *prevailing* winds come, *at that time of year,* in the region where you are, you will know that most hard storms also originate from that direction.

Over most of the continent, almost without fail, a modest wind from the southwest which stays there indicates that counting *from the time it begins,* your chances are good for at least 24 hours of fair weather.

This is regardless of what the barometer is doing. But, the longer it continues, the closer you are to a change and probability of rain. Watch the clouds, and if the southwest wind direction remains constant for three days, you'd better be prepared for bad weather. Tornados generally move from southwest to northeast. This is a severe storm situation, and usually occurs in summer during "thunderstorm weather."

If the wind from the southwest begins to creep around to the west, you can be assured of clear and probably cooler weather for a time. This ordinarily occurs during the bad weather that has come from the southwest, and brings clearing. However, in many areas and at several periods during the year, a wind from the southwest without a storm that moves to the west and keeps right on going to the northwest is telling you that you may get a heavy storm. It might bring one of those early snows, or a driving rain. But a husky blow from the northwest that brings rain or snow, a wind that stays in the northwest or around toward north and whistles right along can be depended upon in most cases to spend itself in one to two days. Following it, clear weather generally appears. A steady, gentle wind from the northwest indicates stable weather for as long as no velocity or direction change occurs.

Probably the most definite sign admonishing you to watch closely and be ready to keep to cover is a wind anywhere from the *east,* anytime of year. Any eastern orientation, from southeast to northeast, invariably means the barometer is falling and that rain or snow is on the way. An east wind is usually damp. From the southeast it will bring rain quite soon. In winter an east wind will probably become higher and carry damp, heavy snow. A storm from the northeast is one of the most miserable; in winter after the storm is finished and when the wind stays there, the cold is bitter and damp.

Conversely, a winter storm from north or northwest may be severe but ordinarily is not as humid or damp, cold but bearable. My rule always is to start hunting cover on a wind from any point of the east. I am also very wary of any shift counterclockwise. This almost certainly indicates bad weather coming.

Natural Signs

In all natural phenomena, no rules are absolute. A friend of mine, a weather hobbyist, says, "You have to remember that weather is *big*, and all over, and can get mixed up." How true!

A ring around moon or sun, for example, is the oldtimer's indication of rain, but that will not always be correct. Nonetheless, there's at least a 60-40 chance. My mother used to tell me stories about an old Irish uncle of hers who was a sailor. He, like thousands of seamen, used the rhyme: "Red sky in the morning, sailors take warning; red sky at night, sailor's delight." This refers to dawn and sunset, and it holds true most of the time.

In the mountains take great care not to misinterpret air currents. In canyons and valleys they are whimsical and do not necessarily indicate steady wind direction. Old mountaineers often say a wind is "blow-ing from every direction" except up on top. During fair spells air current drift in mountains is usually downhill or down-canyon in the forenoon, reversing toward evening. A switch is a clue that a storm may be nearing. Fog that lies low to the ground in canyons at dawn, in crisp air, will usually disappear as the sun rises. A high overcast at dawn may burn off, but keep a check on wind direction and shift. If there is fog *and* drizzle at dawn, prepare for a possible all-day of the same.

Grass wet with dew at dawn presages a pleasant day. Dawns without dew and with the air still and hot but dry, mean you should watch for a storm. Treat frost on grass the same way. If nights are still and each morning there is frost lying everywhere, you can bet the day will at least start off fair and pleasant. But if during frost-time you awake to find none, watch for storms.

Many signs can be misinterpreted. We stated earlier that stratus clouds generally mean rain or snow is shaping up. But you have to check the height of clouds, too. A general rule is that high clouds give you time to anticipate storms, low ones mean hurry up. White clouds are gentle, dark clouds can be mean. Rain clouds moving in on you whose bottoms are shaped like the bottom of an egg carton and are a dirty gray color mean hail is as likely as rain. High, thin stratus clouds commonly appear at dawn even though the previous evening has been clear. They may cover much of the sky. This is not too disturb-ing. Chances are that by nine o'clock they will have dissipated. If you have experienced a bad winter storm, and then the wind from the north or north-west suddenly dies toward sunset, and the sky be-comes clear, this means clearing weather—but it may also mean a real plunge of the thermometer. Get the fire stoked.

Campfire smoke that rises straight up indicates clear weather, but smoke drifting about near the ground probably means an oncoming storm.

There are several other signs all about you in the wilderness that help in anticipating weather. One of the oldest known and checked by woodsmen is what the smoke from a campfire does. If it rises straight up, the weather will be clear. If it is a low smoke shifting helter-skelter, and blowing or drifting close to the ground, it is an almost sure sign of an oncoming storm. Old hands also observe tree leaves on the deciduous trees, during the months previous to their falling. The leaves of all trees in a given area lie naturally with surfaces upward as influenced by the prevailing winds for that region. When leaves show their undersides, you know immediately that this is not a prevailing situation and may well indicate that a storm is on the way.

These and other natural signs are probably not of such practical use to the person in emergency as they are to an outdoorsman who is not under stress. I refer to such phenomena as sounds carrying loudly and for long distances when storms are brewing. There are not very many sounds of consequence that a man lost or stranded in the wilderness is likely to hear. But you might keep in mind that during pre-storm periods, especially when the air is still, you certainly can hear sounds like traffic noises, chopping of a camp axe, a sawmill or chain saw, and others that may mean help, much more plainly than during fair, clear weather. Odors are more easily detected during pre-storm periods. Except for a possible whiff of smoke that may mean help, this too is not very important in my view, so far as survival is concerned. However, there is a bare chance that you may be able to smell game, or certain food plants better at such times.

A common indication of fair weather is the sign of myriad spider webs on grass in the morning. In general, though storms do have profound effects upon wildlife, I do not believe these really help you out of difficulty. That is, you are not likely to see enough of such effects to assist to any extent in forecasting weather.

Animal and Bird Signs

It is interesting nonetheless to observe such signs. Deer, for example, may feed intently before a storm. The trouble is they may also feed intently at any other time. Moose feed heavily previous to a storm, but you are not likely to see any great number of moose, and if a moose is sighted feeding, who knows, it just may be hungry and not the least bit storm conscious. Don't make too much out of these signs. They can be misleading.

In western mountains where they are abundant, however, elk are good weather forecasters during that period in fall just prior to the onset of the bad early-winter storms. They seem to feel such storms on the way and head down from their high meadows toward winter range. Though many writers have touted mule deer as being as infallible a sign as elk in this regard, don't you believe it. Thousands of mule deer do spend their summers up at timberline. And all high-country mule deer do make a vertical migration to lower-altitude winter range. But they seem to have an uncanny feeling for distinguishing between a "freak" early storm and the real onset of winter. Often it takes a lot of snow already on the ground up high to launch the downward migration of mule deer. By the time they're moving, you've already had it! Don't depend on them.

Waterfowl and other migratory birds are a better indication. If in woodcock country, for example, such as New England or the northern Great Lakes region, you discover some morning that woodcock are flushing from all around you as you walk, where none had been the previous evening, be assured that they have tumbled in during the night from farther north. The ground has frozen hard up there and they can't probe with their long bills for earthworms. Cold weather is moving south. Skeins of geese heading south, even in clear weather, should warn you of approaching severe weather. Ducks are not quite as sensitive, but watch them nonetheless.

Mourning doves leave on a southern move in autumn at even the slightest cool spell or approach of storms. Bandtailed pigeons of the Rockies and western Coast Ranges are also extremely sensitive to oncoming storms and fly south in loose groups. However, remember that no wildlife forecasts weather more than a few hours in advance. None is ever as concerned about it as you have to be, and if you spend your time watching the wildlife instead of the clouds and the wind, you are concentrating on the least important matter—so far as *survival* is concerned. A bear, like the proverbial groundhog, may be out of den or going to a den too early or too late. If you tried to predict weather by its antics you'd indeed be wasting your time.

Travel Rules

There are a few more rules concerned with weather that you must obey. When a hard storm is brewing, even if you are not certain but are suspicious, by all means stop where you are. Gather wood, build a shelter. Prepare to ride it out. In spring or summer such storms are not as troublesome or long-lasting as in fall and winter in the northern latitudes, when much snow and severe cold may arrive. Don't try to beat a storm like that. Make yourself as secure and comfortable as you can, and stay right there until the weather changes again. Convince yourself all over again that you are *not in a hurry*. Rushing in this case can kill you!

In hot desert terrain, never travel during the day. Even in searing summer weather the deserts invariably become cool in the evening. When the sun is low, begin your trek. If possible make for a specific destination, one you can reach before full dark. Then, arise in the predawn light and make for another reachable goal, hopefully, before the heat arrives. During desert travel at both times, beware of snakes. They, too, do most of their moving around in the cool periods and at night.

During severe thunderstorms when lightning is crackling nearby, stop immediately, shelter or none, and get low to the ground. Shy adamantly from shelter beneath large, lone trees, or for that matter any tall timber. Low brush or no cover is better, even if you get wet. If you are camped beneath tall trees and a hard thunderstorm rolls in, leave your axe and other metals at camp, grab tarp or rain suit and get into low, dense conifers or brush. Most severe thunderstorms occur during summer anyway, and seldom last long. You can dry out and get warm later.

Violent windstorms are quite common in summer over much of the continent. Most are brief. If you

The best lightning shelter is the lowest cover.
If you are caught in an electrical storm, don't
settle down under a large tree but look for an
open area, stay close to the ground, and still.

are in any water craft, get ashore immediately. On
a lake, keep the prow if at all possible straight into
the wind until you ground. When traveling on water
or land, get away from trees. Stay low in brush, or
beneath rock ledges or comparable cover if you can
possibly reach such a spot. The tornado and cyclone
are something else. Your chances of having to deal
with one, in most regions of this continent where survival situations occur, are not large. A cave or a cut-
bank, with opening facing toward the northwest, or

a deep gully or wash running on a northeast-southeast slant, is the best you can hope for. No one can advise you further. You just have to trust to luck.

In closing, I believe the truly important rules for survival can be summarized very simply. Be sure someone knows where you are going and when you expect to be back. Know how to use both map and compass, and treasure both as your life, which they may well be. On every jaunt, from that impetuous short trek near camp or car to a full-fledged wilderness trip, go prepared materially and mentally for trouble. Know your own country, and study beforehand the facts about strange terrain where you're going. Know your water sources, the wild foods where you'll be, the how-to of fires and shelters. On every trip, even into surrounding fields, constantly practice observation in the outdoors until you see, hear, smell and are aware of everything around you.

Then, if you meet trouble head on, don't buck the weather but bend to its will, for it's always going to do something, such as get better. And, without any question most important of all—keep your cool! Upon those three words depends the successful unraveling of all the problem threads leading to your survival!

Index